MW01174035

Outdoors Guy-

L.O.L

(Loving Outdoor Living)

**Collective Experience Of a
Self-Professed Outdoors Junkie**

**Your Outdoors 101 Guide to
Camping, Fishing, and Survival.**

By Bob Purnell-"Outdoors Guy"

Acknowledgements:

First and foremost, I wish to thank my wife Jayne and my daughter Tracy for always proof reading my articles, noting corrections and offering numerous helpful suggestions.

Thanks to my children Steph, Alison, Karen, and Bob, who, along with Tracy, provided so many happy memories of past family camping trips. These were the trips that developed family traditions. When we returned to the cabin we always re-enacted some special "rituals"- Native North American Day when we crafted villages, and roasted hot dogs over the fire with marshmallows and S'mores for dessert. Hiking trails, swimming at the beach, reading Archie™ comics, and even playing a round of 9-hole golf on a "course" I devised around the cabin. Jayne gets so much credit for all the planning ahead of time. Always having just the right snacks, things to do and read to keep the kids occupied.

Thanks go out to so many knowledgeable authors whose books I've read and learned so much from.

Thanks to the editors of the cottage country newspaper- "Great North Arrow"- Jim Shedden and Cyndi Culbert who

Acknowledgements

welcomed my idea of writing about the outdoors and encouraged me to keep developing my ideas.

Thanks to all the friends I've met camping over the years- the camp fires at night, the stories, the wisecracks, helping each other out when we needed something or just the presence of a friend. After 30 years of going up north to the Teacher's Federation Campsite, I've met so many people, had so much fun, and have banked so many happy times in my memory.

I thank God who instilled in me the passion for the outdoors, gave me a wonderful family, an amazing teaching career (where I could "try out" my ideas in the classroom to enhance outdoors and survival units we worked on in the curriculum), and so many occasions to get out and enjoy the outdoors.

*"Great North Arrow" is a cottage country newspaper based in Dunchurch, Ontario which reaches a monthly readership of 6 500. My monthly column, "Outdoors Guy" has run for 2 years now and the idea to collect and publish these articles in an organized fashion is what provided the stimulus for this book. I am so proud to write for this amazing publication. *The name of this publication, my "Outdoors Guy" column name, and the editors' names are used with their kind permission.

Introduction:

This book presents a collection of articles stemming from 50 years of learning about the outdoors. I took to fishing as a kid from the first time I went out with the bobber, hook, and worm. I still remember the day when my mail-order package arrived form (then) Simpson's Sears with my first spin cast set and a few lures.

Fishing has been a 50 year learning curve for me. After doing numerous things the wrong way and wondering how I could get results, I began to read fishing magazines and books. I began to watch fishing shows. The day I discovered spinners as a universally effective lure represented a leap. Fishing buddies taught me how to fish for trout and salmon. My wife bought me a beautiful, complete fly fishing beginner's set one Christmas and my summer adventures at a trout club began. With better knowledge came much more consistent success.

One day I happened to notice a pamphlet on the table in the school lunch room. It showed pictures of a beautiful campsite owned by the Ontario Teacher's Federation. This was back in 1985. We went up for 4 days and practically got frozen out. But we went back, year after year. Ever since I was a child, watching one of my favourite TV shows, "Hawkeye", I dreamed about

Introduction

adventures in the outdoors. Again, it was a learning experience. Reading, trying out my own ideas, always finding more information.

Finally, as a natural soul mate to my passion for camping came learning about survival. I was, literally, fascinated by the techniques of bush craft, especially shelter building. My last year of teaching gave me a fabulous class who loved to learn. During a unit on survival (which offered mostly information about natural disasters and little about actually surviving), I decided to try teaching actual outdoors skills to the students. For a week we talked about shelters, fires, cooking, first aid, signaling, keeping warm, navigating, and organizing a camp. As a surprise, my students walked in on the last day before Christmas, got divided into 4 groups, and were given the tasks of cooking, signaling, building a make shift shelter, and a fire pit (all <u>simulated</u>, of course.) I provided them with materials from my survival and camping supplies. My best actress high-lighted the scene by pretending to break her ankle, which meant that the signaling group had to calm her down, administer first aid and still continue attempting to attract rescuers. This activity took the whole morning. The kids had a BLAST! I'll never forget it. One of my tech savvy Grade 7's used a smart phone application to simulate a fire for cooking. Young adults have a world of creative energy and imagination. Why not provide the outdoors as a life-long opportunity for them

This book isn't an exhaustive treatise on the outdoors. It is meant to be simple, useful, and fun. I've learned from so many others, but I've also tried a host of my own ideas as well. It's one of the things that makes the outdoors, well, infinitely discoverable.

It continually draws a person. There is ALWAYS a new project to try, a new challenge, a new idea. And then there's just the feeling that you're returning "home"-that this is your happy place.

No technique in this book comes with a 100% guarantee because no two situations in the outdoors are ever exactly the same. Be aware first, and able to anticipate. But you'll learn many tips, strategies and techniques to increase your odds and help you just plain enjoy your outdoors adventures more.

You'll hear me say a lot about two things in this book. 1. SAFETY overrides every other consideration-whether on the water, the road, in snow, or at a campsite. Respect nature and use your common sense. There simply is no substitute for proper and extensive planning ahead of time and for ALWAYS establishing and consistently following safety procedures. Better to take simple steps to avoid danger than to all of a sudden have to remedy it! 2. Improvisation. You'd be amazed at what you can do with the simplest materials if you have to improvise. The article on coat hangers is one such example. The articles on scavenging and an improvised camp take this many steps further by providing ideas related to practically all aspects of setting up a basic camp with a view of protection (from sun, heat, cold, bugs, and rain), water, camp furnishings, how to cook, create a fire, and provide a few comforts as well. A universal question such as, "What do I do to keep warm and dry without a tent or a sleeping bag?" should have several answers based on your ability to adapt and improvise. Essentially, "I have this equipment, what can I make out of it?" A space blanket can be used as a blanket to keep you warm, but it can also be a reflector to attract rescuers, a tarp to keep rain and wind out of a lean-to, and a rain catcher, when spread out, to collect water. Large garbage bags can be filled with leaves to create a makeshift mattress, a sleeping bag, temporary roof for a shelter, and waterproof covering for equipment and your wood supply. (Get creative!)

The continuation of what this book offers lies with you. There is no limit in the outdoors. Try your own ideas when you've learned an awareness of safety and have learned some ideas that have been tried and tested. You can do it! We all require an outlet for our creativity. The outdoors is the ultimate outlet.

Mostly, though, have fun. Imagine you've got this 1 go around at life and NOW is your opportunity to get out there and learn and experience. Bring a camera and share the experience with family and friends. Enjoy the book. Please make your own notes. This book is presented with the sincere hope that you'll find lots of practical and useful information.

One final note: I have written about the outdoors because I've tried these ideas and techniques out myself. The photos in this book are my own pictures of projects and strategies that I have actually used. Granted, some "projects", (like being stranded by the side of the road in the winter) may never have to be used. You don't have to put yourself deliberately in harm's way to say you've "experienced" something. Much of the information in this book is about NOT having to make the best of a bad situation that could have been avoided. A lot of other information deals with preparation and equipment that will give you many more tools to work with (and thus many more options) in the event of a challenging unforeseen event.

I acknowledge that there is some repetition in this book. Several tools and techniques fit under several headings. The hobo stove fits under the headings of Camping and Survival because you can use it for several things. Please allow me some redundancy. I have tried to reduce it to a minimum.

Nothing is more exciting than learning. Matched with the call of the wild, and accompanied by information and equipment, you have something you can go back to that will always offer adventures and happy (sometimes even "I'll look back on this and laugh someday".) memories. Enjoy the book, then get out there and learn tons more and experience it all.

Outdoors Guy

NOTE: I wish to point out that I've attempted to use the Trade Mark™ symbol for any commercial brand names- especially lures and fishing equipment manufacturers. If there are any missing symbols, I apologize. My effort in this book is to respect brand names. My experience with many brand name products has been that they've really earned their reputation- hence they should be acknowledged.

Table of Contents

Camping:

Fishing:

Survival:

Camping

Coat Hanger = Multi-Tool

In this issue we'll be starting to look at the art of improv-situations where ordinary items can be adapted to perform simple, basic tasks at a campsite. It's important to remember that camping and survival are always about "the basics" if you're the type of person who likes the wilder, rougher side of the outdoors. This issue will focus mostly on cooking. Let's assume you've caught a few panfish and want to have some toast…

A very useful and versatile tool is a coat hanger. (It has to be metal for our purposes.) Here are a few things you can fashion from it.

1. MAKES A HANDY TOASTER. Extend the wire out so you've got a large oval. Then, just create an accordion pattern with one end overlapping the other so as to neatly fit a slice of bread between the metal ridges. Use the hook in the coat hanger as the handle and wear a glove to further help shield your hand from heat. Bingo… toast. You can even, with a little imagination, bend this into a handy potato masher.

2. FRY PAN. Here you want to make a circle out of the hoop part of the hanger. Wrap a layer or 2 of aluminum foil around the outside of the circle and pinch/crimp the foil down as much as you can so the foil will hold. Works well provided you don't load it up too heavily. Now have a good, quick fish fry over a fire. Remember to use oil, butter, margarine, etc. so you're not scraping the thin surface of the foil and therefore breaking it. Alternately, just make a round frame to support an aluminum pie pan. Crimp the sides of the pie pan around the wire frame. An aluminum pie pan is much sturdier than crimped foil.

3. THE CLASSIC SPIT STICK. Set up a couple of "y" sticks on either side of a small fire. I always prefer a tepee type fire- easiest to make and the updraft of air feeds the flames and will burn even damp wood. Undo the coat hanger so that you have a long wire with a handle then brace it with your fish, hot dogs, (rattlesnakes…), on the "spit". You can then rotate your delicacy to cook it even on all sides. The heavier gauge wire- the better. *Watch the size of your fire! Small is better so you don't hurt yourself. You can then put it out more easily afterwards assuming you only needed the fire for cooking and not for other purposes.

4. HERE'S A "GAFF"- BEND THE LOOP IN THE COAT HANGER AND IMPROVISE A GAFF FOR FISHING. I certainly wouldn't try this for monster-sized fish, but let's assume you forgot your net and need something extra to help coax a resistant fish into your boat.

5. POTATO MASHER -TWIST THE WIRES TO FORM AN IMPRO-VISED POTATO MASHER. You have the handle already.

6. TENT PEGS- In a pinch- cut off and shape some Improv tent pegs.

Outdoors Guy

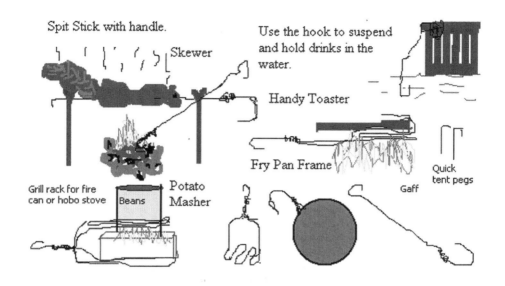

Spit Stick with handle.

Skewer

Use the hook to suspend and hold drinks in the water.

Handy Toaster

Fry Pan Frame

Quick tent pegs

Grill rack for fire can or hobo stove

Beans

Potato Masher

Gaff

Water Filtration and Hobo Stove/Heater

Water Filtration: Let's say you are outdoors and need to assure that you have safe drinking water. You can NEVER assume that because water looks clear that it's safe. After all, bacteria are too small to see. Added to this, the water may be cloudy, contain debris, or be outright dirty. Here's a method to try to filter water that I've used myself.

Cut the top off of a 2 litre pop bottle. Rinsed and dried out it makes a very handy funnel- even for pouring oil into your car's engine. That's not what we're using it for in this situation. Invert the top over the body of the bottle and you have a funnel with a catch bottle. Now, take a coffee filter or 2 (even a paper napkin, paper towel, hand towel, etc.), add some beach sand (the whiter the better), and grind up about 3 tablespoons of charcoal. (By the way- make SURE that the charcoal wasn't taken from a poisonous tree.) Maple is my favourite (smells nice.) Now shake the sand and charcoal together until mixed evenly.

Next step is important- if you can. Run water thru the filter to "rinse" it. You'll be able to tell when the water clears. If the water you're filtering is dirty, may as well just start right away- the result will be better than drinking muddy water. Then it's ready to filter your water. Pour water thru the filter slowly enough that dirty water does rise above the level of your paper- otherwise you'll just be pouring dirty water into your container. The sand/charcoal/paper filter will remove most particles.

Finally, BOIL the water you've filtered for a few minutes or add 1 drop of bleach per litre of filtered water to kill bacteria. Swish it around and let stand for an hour so that the chlorine has a chance to work effectively.

* Please note that makeshift strategies are never 100% foolproof. In a survival situation you are always aiming for the best you can make out of a situation. Safety precautions and common sense come first. Boiling water that appears clear is one such example.

Hobo Stove:

This is a handy item to cook with and serves as a heater in colder weather. You can even consider it for use to warm your hands while ice fishing.

Start with a coffee can- (metal- of course...). Add 1/2 to an inch of sand to the bottom. Now, punch holes in the can all the way around just above the level of the sand inside to provide a supply of oxygen to the fire. Now you add some fire starters, coals, briquettes etc. (which may be found even at dollar stores). Be careful lighting these! My preference is to buy fast-igniting "fire-starters" and use a barbecue lighter (with a LONG handle). Once you have the coals lit, it should burn evenly for a while and provide heat. Add a grill rack (I got several at garage sales) onto the top of the coffee can and you can now cook. Bending a coat hanger into shape can make an improvised grill rack, and even a "toaster".

Important to Consider: I always have an aluminum pie pan under the can to ensure that what I've set it on doesn't catch fire. Secondly- watch how much fuel you're burning- you don't need a raging fire that you may not be able to control or even put out quickly. Use just a coal or 2- not even flaming. Make sure that the fire or ember is COMPLETELY OUT and that the can is cool. Use water or sand as usual for dousing camp fires. In the event you are in an improvised emergency shelter, build a barrier between yourself and the stove and place the pie pan under it. It only has to keep you warm, (take the edge off) not to burn your shelter down.

Rule of Thumb- you have to be able to regulate and control anything you've ignited- start slowly. Of course, keep the heat well away from direct contact with flammable materials in your emer-gency shelter. If the shelter is enclosed be careful. Combustion uses large amounts of oxygen. A strategy is to use a hollow tube from birch bark as an air inlet at the base of the shelter and then to have another such tube as a chimney. Falling asleep with the can still actively producing heat is asking for trouble. You have to tend anything burning. Hopefully, you'll have time to bed down in something warm having taken the edge off of your chill and having made sure the flame is out.

 *Safety- <u>FIRST</u>!!

Outdoors Guy

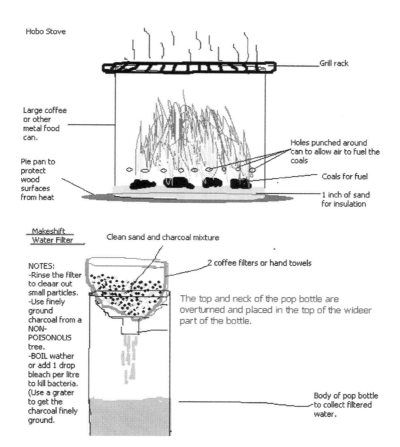

Hobo Stove

Grill rack

Large coffee or other metal food can.

Holes punched around can to allow air to fuel the coals

Pie pan to protect wood surfaces from heat

Coals for fuel

1 inch of sand for insulation

Makeshift Water Filter

Clean sand and charcoal mixture

2 coffee filters or hand towels

NOTES:
-Rinse the filter to cleaar out small particles.
-Use finely ground charcoal from a NON-POISONOUS tree.
-BOIL wather or add 1 drop bleach per litre to kill bacteria. (Use a grater to get the charcoal finely ground.

The top and neck of the pop bottle are overturned and placed in the top of the wideer part of the bottle.

Body of pop bottle to collect filtered water.

The Art of Camp Cooking a la Improv

Welcome back to Outdoors Guy. I want my articles to keep in time with the season changing. Lots of us folks will be going camping soon, so this month we discuss ways to "rough it" with cooking. Some of these ideas require little space and equipment. Here goes…

1. Simplest. Use an empty tuna can. Wind cardboard inside it until the space inside is completely filled. Drip wax over the cardboard, let it cool, and you have an improvised mini stove. Place a pie pan or cookie sheet underneath to insulate the hot can from the picnic table or log you may be cooking on. Next, shape a coat hanger to form a grill rack over the can. On top of this ultra-high tech contraption, place one can of beans (or whatever...) A more stable arrangement is to place a small grill rack between two bricks and place the bean can on the rack. Open the bean can almost all the way around so the lid can be bent over. Use pliers to hold the lid when lifting or moving it. CAREFUL! **<u>NEVER</u>** touch the lid with bare hands. Use pliers and even leather gloves. The metal is sharp. I've found the best and easiest way to extinguish the flame when you're done is to simply place a pie pan over the can. Then LET IT COOL COMPLETELY. Ahhhh beans...

2. Chocolates Tin Stove: Save those old chocolate cans- those last-minute gifts for Christmas (shallow ones work best). Open one and place 1/2 inch of sand in the bottom (insulation so you don't burn the picnic table). Place a few fire starter coals on the sand and light them. Just like my dad's old fashioned barbecue- waiting for the briquettes to catch. Over top place a grill rack and cook. When done, this should be allowed to completely cool and the coals burn out. Cover and re-use later.

3. Hobo Stove: A real classic. Use a large METAL coffee tin, place an inch of sand in the bottom, then again, coals on

the sand. This is the tricky part…you have to punch lots of holes in a ring around the side of the can JUST at the level of the coals to feed the fire with air. Add a grill rack to the top and cook. These can come in very handy also if you're ice fishing and need a small hand warmer. This is a stove, so DON'T try and use it in a tent as a heater. OR…turn it over, cut a vent for air, put a pie pan underneath, light some coals, and use the top flat, shiny surface for frying.

4. Fire Grill: (Small, so as to control heat and flames/sparks.) You can use concrete blocks to support a grill rack on both sides of a campfire.

5. Spit Rack: Use 2 "Y" sticks on either side of a teepee fire to support a spit stick in the middle. Use a coat hanger or some type of non-poisonous wood (apple, cherry, hickory, alder are all used to smoke meat because of their flavour). (Here he goes with the coat hanger again, but think about it…The coat hanger gives you a handle to turn your meat.) Fish wrapped in foil can be secured in the middle of the spit stick. Turn regularly.

6. Hot Coals: I imagine everyone's done this. Wait for the fire to die down to embers and then toss a few spuds, individually wrapped into the coals. With some butter, maybe onions, salt, pepper, cheese, bacon, (use your imagination and individual taste) you can create a baked potato, poutine, whatever. You can also cook fish in this way, but check it. The meat is done when the flesh "flakes" and the fish should be wrapped with oil, margarine, (lemon, onion, beer). Not dry.

7. Anchored Skewer: Set up a "Y" stick beside your camp-fire and place a marshmallow skewer/coat hanger/stick with bark removed on an angle- leaning on the "Y" stick, with whatever you want to roast over the heat. With a coat hanger or long enough marshmallow skewer, you can cook 2 hotdogs at once. Use 2 or 3 of these rigs to keep the hotdogs coming if you're feeding the troops! Let's see…4 of these anchored skewers times 2 hotdogs each… 8 at a time. Should keep 'em munching. (When the kids are busy eating, they're QUIET, right?) Just don't let them near the fire. You're the adult and the chef.

So there you have it- some simple outdoors type chef ideas. (Some camp recipes guaranteed to produce heart burn follow up this article. For now, take time to "digest" the present mate-rial.) Please remember- **<u>SAFETY FIRST</u>**. Control your heat, watch sparks, extinguish any flame or live coals **<u>COMPLETELY</u>**.

*If anyone has some good camp cooking recipes or other im-provised cooking ideas, please contact me at the e-mail address. Hope you've enjoyed this one! See you next month.

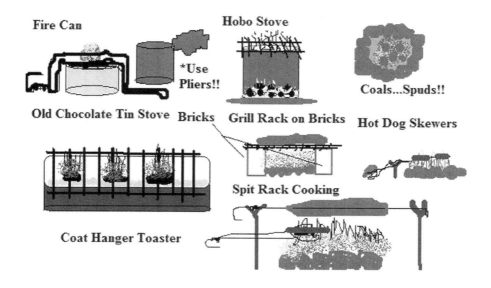

Fire Can

Hobo Stove

*Use Pliers!!

Coals...Spuds!!

Old Chocolate Tin Stove Bricks Grill Rack on Bricks Hot Dog Skewers

Spit Rack Cooking

Coat Hanger Toaster

The Saga Continues-Improv I

This promises to be a good issue- Odds 'n' Ends. Let me start out by saying nothing substitutes for preparation- training and knowledge, equipment. Imagine leaving home to travel up into Muskoka or Rainbow Country with no booster cables, flares, emergency flares, first-aid kit, candles, matches, energy bars, water, an emergency blanket, tools or cell phone. "Nothing's going to happen". Usually it doesn't. The question begs- what are you going to do if the vehicle breaks down, visibility is poor and road conditions are treacherous? I saw a couple in a station wagon almost plough into the exit sign (Route 117 near Bracebridge) in heavy snow- a little misjudgment of road conditions and speed?

Perhaps- if they'd hit the median between the highway and the exit ramp they'd have been in trouble. We're so fortunate to be living in an age of amazing technology- cell phones, GPS systems, Personal Locator Beacons, etc. It makes everything sound so easy and convenient.

I'm not in love with dispensing with high-tech gear for the sake of "real outdoor survival". The technology is available. Get it. Use it!! Getting back to where I started, there's also nothing like preparing- have equipment, know how to use it, plan a route, inform at least 2 other people where you're going so it's easier to track you down. Usually, the best plan if you're stuck is to stay put. If you veer too far off the path- now you're in an unknown location- and harder to find.

All this having been said- there will be situations where we have to take stock of what we have- and improvise. Here are a few ideas at random to illustrate the idea of improvising:

1. In another article we discuss the humble orange garbage bag. Here's a thought. PFD's are orange for a reason. It's visible. So, you may not have a life jacket. You may be able to improvise with an orange garbage bag. If you tread water for a few seconds, open the garbage bag and fill it (almost) with air, then securely seal it by tying it. Hopefully it has no holes or you'll be getting a rather sinking feeling about the situation. (*Please refer to the Garbage Bag article for further detail.)

2. Finally he gets away from the garbage bag. (I can hear a few people saying, "Yay!" to this.) You want to rake up some leaves for bedding. Snap! Tie a few braches with plenty of twigs on their tips. Handy broom/rake.

3. My greatest invention! Dryer lint loosely packed in toilet paper rolls. This stuff goes up like crazy for starting fires. Be **<u>CAREFUL</u>**!! Sap from balsam fir trees (they have pockets of sap in the bark) burns well too. You need to collect a fair bit of it.

4. Detergent/vegetable oil jugs. Rinse out, fill with sand and attach a rope around the handle. You now have a makeshift anchor. It may also make a fun toy for the kids if thoroughly rinsed. Make scoops to play scoop ball with. The scoop can also serve as a handy bailing bucket with a handle already conveniently attached.

5. "Bill, the drain in the sink/shower (at the cottage) is plugged!" You may try untwisting a coat hanger and using the coiled end as a makeshift snake to get hair out of a drain. I've done it. It really worked. *Make a small "hook" in the twisted end with needle-nose pliers.

6. Pie pans are fry pans. Use pliers to handle- please. They can also be used for signaling. In addition, you can combine an aluminum pie pan with a coat hanger frame to make a pretty decent fry pan. (*See article #1)

7. Birch bark- used in an emergency to splint a fracture if no newspaper or magazines or triangular bandages are handy. (Not on open skin!!) You can write on it to leave directions for followers.

8. Freeze a few water bottles before leaving. They could be used as ice packs.

9. Here's a gourmet one. No grill. Hmmmmmm.... Want to cook that fish. Here's an idea.

Take 2 "Y" sticks and place them at opposite ends of a small fire. I prefer a teepee fire- gets hot- keep it small. Find a piece of green wood (not poisonous!), strip off the bark, (even wet it) and it will be ready to be the spit. Now...line the stick with foil (heavy duty). We assume the fish is gutted and scaled. Stuff the innards with onion, lemon, lime wedges, salt, pepper, garlic powder, an ounce of beer, etc. (Everybody's got a pet recipe.) Make sure to oil/margarine the layer of aluminum foil that you'll be wrapping around the fish. Now lay the fish's gutted stomach (that you've put the flavouring in) along the spit stick and wrap several times with aluminum foil. I doubt this work with a real monster- but it's worth a try with panfish. My thought is to use an outside layer of foil like the folks at a hamburger fast food place would- fold one edge over another a few times and crimp the ends around the stick. You now have what looks like, in effect, an aluminum hot dog. Place over the fire suspended between the 2 "Y" sticks and turn to cook evenly.

10. I wouldn't do this with a metal canoe with lightning nearby. We're out fishing in a canoe. It starts pouring or it soon will. Abandon all notions of pike biting well in the rain. We may have forgotten our garbage bags (Mercy!!). You have time to get to shore and have to improvise- QUICKLY. Turn the canoe over (or if possible place at least one end on a log to elevate, and drape a tarp over the side to form a makeshift shelter). Carrying mosquito netting would be of primary importance if you're on a canoe trip. Have <u>plenty</u> of it! Drape a combination of netting and tarp over the side. Now how about a bit of comfort? This leads me to my next idea.

11. I <u>have</u> forgotten a sleeping mat in my years of camping. A good trip <u>always</u> entails forgetting something! (Said tongue in cheek!) So I used kneeling pads and life jackets as a makeshift "mattress". Not the most comfortable mattress, but better than the ground.

13. That baking soda used to help lessen the effects of stings can also be improvised to brush your teeth and extinguish a fire. I always have a box at home near the stove and have used it- a large hand full thrown directly on the stove fire.

14. The lowly coat hanger can be twisted to form a primitive grill rack over your hobo stove, used in pieces for makeshift tent pegs, or even to hang up fish from a clothesline to keep predators from stealing your prize.

15. Here's an idea: In deep snow- tie pine or spruce branches to your boots to distribute your weight and stay on top of the snow. I used to walk into Science class with badminton racquets on my feet to show the kids Improv snow shoes- and also to show Pressure = Force / Area. Maybe old tennis racquets would work??? Remember to lay flat on ice if it's weakening- same principle.

*I'll repeat- <u>nothing</u> replaces being prepared. Anticipate what should be packed on a trip. Being tuck in a blizzard or in the bush without equipment is no romantic notion. Travelling should always involve a quality first aid kit and roadside kit. That cigarette lighter cell phone charger may be a life saver. Improvisation is for when you have to figure out what to do or make with what you've got to accomplish a specific task. Better not to have to improvise at all if you are equipped to deal with a situation yourself and/or get help quickly. Be Safe! Plan ahead.

Outdoors Guy

The Art of Improv II- What You CAN Do With A Coffee Can

The coffee can. What an enabling instrument. Let's get the irritation over with first. The kids are playing the drums with them and it's driving you MENTAL! Got this one covered. Gently introduce them to ways in which a coffee can may be practical and useful. Tell them you'll get them some beach toys to play with because, "…we need those cans for other things."

Think about storage ("store-age") like you've got a store and need lots of space. Use the coffee cans to store dry foods like rice, pasta, beans, raisins, granola, flour, and dried soups, juice crystals. Use smaller cans for salt, sugar, bread crumbs and spices.

The most efficient foods to pack for survival or long term camping are dried foods- the most food for the least space. Large coffee cans are ideal for storage and labelling. They also allow you to buy in bulk since you're storing in bulk.

Large coffee cans are also handy to store emergency candles, first aid supplies, batteries, wash cloths, utensils, and as sealed canisters to keep toilet paper rolls safe from mice.

Now for some campfire uses: Take a large metal coffee can and a coat hanger. Punch a hole under the top lip of the coffee can on 2 opposite sides. Now hook the coat hanger into the holes exactly like a paint-can design. You now not only have a pot, but one which can be suspended for cooking (for example: suspended from a tripod). You can also just use the can as a pot in its own right.

This is one of my "greatest inventions" (at least I like to think so…). Use 2 large coffee or pasta sauce cans to create a meat smoker. One can (the eventual bottom one) should have both top and bottom lids removed so that it's basically a hollow cylinder. Now you have to CAREFUL with the next step. Cut a "mouse hole" (best way I can think of describing it) into the wall of the can- less than ½ way up the side. It's an upside down "U". This is to allow air to circulate to your coals and create an up draft.

Can #2 simply needs to have holes punched in the bottom. Now let's put this together.

The bottom can is placed on a pie pan on which you've placed glowing coals. On top of the glowing coals are wood chips from an aromatic tree like apple, alder, mesquite, hickory, or maple. My fave mixture is ¼ apple, ¼ cherry, and ½ hickory. These wood chips are available commercially from outdoors stores. Place chips are available commercially from outdoors stores. Place chips on the coals (briquettes are easiest to do this with and burn the longest) and then place the mouse hole can over the chips/coals. Take a grill rack with thinly sliced meat/fillets and place the grill rack on top of the mouse hole can. Then take can #2 and place it upside down on the grill rack. Smoke escapes out of the holes punched in the top, but not before it has a chance to flavour your meat. Salted meat or brined and dried meat will last longer (and likely taste better). Smoking is a good way to help preserve the "shelf-life" of your meat.

Now to really go from the "Camping" scenario to the "Survival" scenario... A large coffee can or 2 can be a lifesaver because they can hold some VERY NECESSARY survival gear in a small space. Get creative here and think about what the most necessary items are based on what you need to survive in an emergency.

Warmth: Emergency candles made especially for survival or at least 5 or 6 normal candles. 3 ways to start a fire- lighters (plural), matches and a Magnifying glass which may also be helpful removing splinters & stingers. Carry 1 space blanket (mylar) for each person in your vehicle. Hand warmers are a good choice for a compact source of heat.

Rain/Wind/Bugs/Sunlight: Orange garbage bags (you knew this was coming...), a portable rain poncho (1 per person), mosquito netting (at least a hood), bug repellent & sunscreen.

Energy: Have a metal cup packed with trail bars, dried soup packets, bullion packets. A hexamine stove is small, compact, and comes with fire starters.

Water Filtration: Pack the top of a pop bottle with some coffee filters to help clean water. (*See article #2- Water Filtration and Hobo Stove)

Miscellaneous: A folding knife (THE MUST-HAVE ITEM in a survival kit!), 50 ft. of strong string, flashlight (spare batteries if it's battery powered or a wind up flashlight that doesn't require batteries). A signal mirror or- just as good- a CD, a couple of charcoal briquettes, small pie pan, a whistle, and a small multi tool.

Believe it or not, all this stuff CAN be packed in a large coffee can. I've done it.

In the spirit of the above survival emphasis, consider also using the coffee can to boil water once you've filtered it. The can may be used for signaling both visually (shine it), and as an auditory signal (bang on it if you think rescuers are approaching). It can also be used to contain a small fire to help keep you warm. (*See Article #2 again- Hobo Stove)

One last thought: At Christmas, why not fill your own survival coffee can with a few changes like a hat/mitts/socks in exchange for the water filtration equipment, knife and CD. Add some cookies, some tea bags, some candy and a card "From a Friend Who Cares". In areas where homeless people are on the streets, this would make such a great gift. The Salvation Army will distribute them for you. Believe me; they know who needs them.

All this, with just a large coffee can.

I'll say it: "YES, YOU...<u>CAN</u>!"

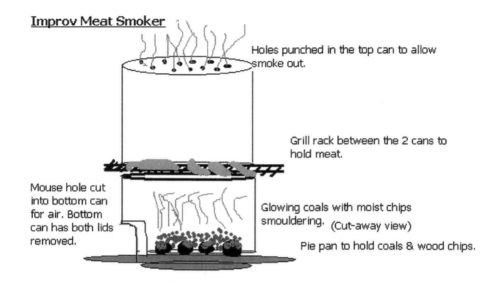

Improv Meat Smoker

Holes punched in the top can to allow smoke out.

Grill rack between the 2 cans to hold meat.

Mouse hole cut into bottom can for air. Bottom can has both lids removed.

Glowing coals with moist chips smouldering. (Cut-away view)

Pie pan to hold coals & wood chips.

The Art of Improv III- Some First Aid Plus...

This article was meant to be a companion to "Art of Improv II", which started out with the kids banging on coffee cans with sticks. OK. We did the coffee can thing- let's now take their sticks away too and get them their beach toys (this is more applicable than you might think...wait until we need one of their beach toys...).

I'd like to begin with something that GREW (not grows) on trees- dead birch bark. If someone has to have a limb immobilized on the trail due to a fracture or sprain, use birch bark as a splint. Tie off with rope, a belt or 2, or duct tape. Make sure the splint isn't too tight- the casualty shouldn't be losing feeling and circulation to the affected limb. Loosen and re- tie if necessary. Monitor the person and keep warm or in the shade as weather dictates.

Now for the sticks: Here's my first improv suggestion. Find a sturdy (about an inch to 1 ½ inches thick) stick/branch with a "Y" in it. Cut the "Y" stick to fashion a makeshift crutch- bonus points if another branch can be cut off further down the branch and used as a handle. Tailor the length of the stick to the height of your casualty. Pad the crotch of the "Y" with a jacket or T-shirt for comfort.

If this is a hiking scenario, I'd suggest bringing a couple of bottles of frozen water. Ice applied for the first 15 minutes can greatly sooth pain and swelling, With the ice frozen solid in a water bottle, they're be some ice available again in an hour for re-icing the sprain.

Cold water is also a critical first measure against heat exhaustion. Hope fully you've stopped and are resting a person BEFORE heat stroke happens. Be careful!! Have a person sit down and apply cold compresses. You have to get their skin temperature cooled off. Keep at it as long as necessary. Call for help. Take Basic First Aid so you'll know what to do.

Now for those strong branches… You can improvise a travois with two longer branches and by lashing some cross pieces. Pad with jackets and a blanket. Similarly, roll a blanket or 2 between two long, straight poles and improvise a stretcher (likely some re-inforcement will be needed to hold the blanket in place). Several large beach towels may be even better. This idea may serve you well if help isn't immediately available and you have to get out of the scene of an accident or injury. *Be careful that the blanket/towels don't unroll- dropping your casualty to the ground! **A SERIOUS NOTE!! Spinal injury is serious and the casualty has to be properly immobilized. If you can, at all, let the professionals do this. In most cases, with necessary precautions and some equipment, a person can be kept stable and comfortable enough until qualified personnel arrive and take over. PLEASE: Take Basic First Aid!!

In the same vein as a travois, you can improvise a ladder. My suggestion is to slant the 2 upright poles in an angle- narrower at the top. This helps prevent the rungs from slipping after you lash them onto the ladder. Use thick, sturdy uprights and cross pieces! Best to notch the uprights at regular intervals where you will be lashing your cross pieces. Narrowing the ladder towards the top helps make the lashings more secure.

Please note the previous articles on camp furniture and Improv I for using sticks to design furniture (the swamp bed and the platform bed, the camp bench…). That way I can go on, without undue repetition to…

The Tripod: I used it this year for cooking and will combine it with a coffee can and coat hanger so I'm keeping my premise of doing what I suggest myself. The tripod can also become a tipi, or even a set of improv shelves. I suspended my camp pot from my tripod with a bungee cord or a fish chain. Beans were never so…"outdoorsy". (NO…I DIDN'T burn them!! They were good!) BTW…use a pair of pliers to help handle the pot!

OK. Poor kids… it's take their stuff time again. I really don't think they'd mind. Someone with a suspected fracture requires a splint. You can use a child's water wings as a more comfortable alternative to, let's say, wood slats. It's also easily adjustable!

This may be unrelated (wood-wise) but we're talking about improvised first aid. The plantain plant is easily recognized by the large veins which run from the stalk all the way along the leaves to their tips. This may be smashed up (or even chewed) and used as a aid to calming down a minor skin rash. It's a natural healing plant (as well as a source of food).

Enough "Improv" for a while… Like so many other articles, this has the tone of see if you can make use of a combination of what you've brought and what you can find.

FINAL NOTE: HAVE a first aid kit!! A GOOD one!!!! No sense having to take a course in medicinal herbs if you have the right ointments, etc. ALWAYS clean and sterilize/cover an open wound. Nothing substitutes for First Aid training. Best to KNOW you know what to do.

Safe Journeys. The "Art of the Improv" isn't just for the stage- when camping you do it all the time…

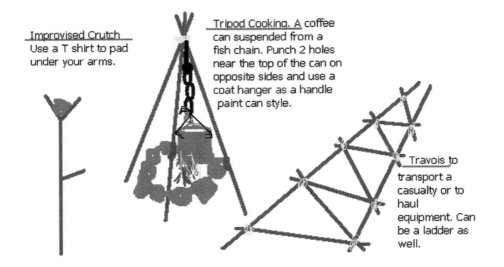

Improvised Crutch
Use a T shirt to pad under your arms.

Tripod Cooking. A coffee can suspended from a fish chain. Punch 2 holes near the top of the can on opposite sides and use a coat hanger as a handle paint can style.

Travois to transport a casualty or to haul equipment. Can be a ladder as well.

Totally Improv Camp

This is definitely for the real outdoors types. Please use any idea you wish should you happen to forget something. Assume you've brought no mattress, no tent, no mosquito net, no pillow. You are the TRUE outdoors person. (Or an incurably cheap person…) You like to "rough it". You are back in the pioneer and fur trade days. Great! This article may even cure you.

We begin with some uses for a larger tarp and then a smaller one. The small tarp is your ground sheet to keep you away from bugs and moisture. The larger tarp will perform the task of being your shelter, and you get to choose your style of accommodations. You can have a lean-to, tent, teepee, or even bunk under your canoe- a true voyageur. Owing to the space and scope of this topic, for now I'll be talking about an "A-frame" tarp tent and canoe shelter. (More to come in the future…) Here's how to start building an Improv Camp.

To fashion a tent, simply find 4 sturdy sticks about half the circumference of your wrist. These will form your "A-frame" back and front door for your tent. This tent can be made simply by just using 1 long rope. Lash the branches together in pairs. They'll be the frames for the front and back doors. Now peg down one end of the rope and run it over the top of the first A-frame pair of sticks. Run a ridgeline from the back "A" to the front "A", around the top of front "A", and then down on an angle and peg it down. (*See diagram) It's a good idea to run the rope around the top of both "A"s for added stability. Now simply drape the tarp over the ridgeline between the 2 "A"s and peg down to the ground thru the grommets on the sides of the tarp. If the lines are taut, this is actually quite wind-resistant and secure. So you have a home now. Note that, if your groundsheet is laying further out than your actual tent (it goes under the edges of the tent and is open on the ground) then rain can pool on the outside edges of the tarp and run into the tent. It is best to have the groundsheet just INSIDE the floor dimensions of the tent. (*A variation on this design is to rig up your tarp in A-Frame fashion above the ground- suspended between two trees as a shade for your bed, chair, or hammock. Simply anchor the tarp to the ground with rope tied thru the side grommets and pegs. (*See the tarp diagram.) Obviously, the larger the tarp you have, the more living space you'll have. "Just think… We have a bigger tarp than the neighbours." Now we have to outfit it.

Use a large garbage bag like you would to collect all the leaves you've raked from your lawn in the fall. Stuff as many <u>dry</u> leaves into it as you can, sit on it, compress the leaves, and then go and stuff some more <u>dry</u> leaves into the bag. You now have a mattress. Note that leaves do flatten out and you'll likely have to add more later on. Lay a blanket over top and then lay your sleeping bag on the blanket. Cosy... Brag about the bargain price you paid for a mattress and move on.

Wouldn't you love a new pillow to match your new mattress? Stuff some more leaves into a smaller shopping bag. Now tie off the end of the pillow so the stuffing remains inside. Place the pillow inside a T-shirt so it's softer and you're not resting your face on cold plastic. You'll also breathe more safely if you sleep prone with your head buried face-first in the pillow. (*Mentioned in the garbage bag article as well.)

Now we have to keep out the mosquitoes and black flies. This is my idea inspired by taking down old drapes. The sheers were going to be thrown out anyway. Why not use them over the front and back entrances of your tent as bug-netting? Fasten with clothes pegs. NOT hard to undo when you have to make that 2 a.m. bathroom dash either.

So we have floor, mattress, pillow, rain resistant walls, mosquito netting. An important point to note, if you want to keep warm and dry, is that the back end of the tent can be dropped right to the ground in the event of heavy winds and rain. (Called a "Quick Shelter") Study which way the prevailing winds are coming from. You don't want to create a wind tunnel which might chill you to the bone. You also don't want the open parts of the tent open facing a lashing rain. Try to have the sides or the back of the tent facing the wind or the back end dropped down <u>facing into the wind</u>. I haven't forgotten about the front opening. You just may need an extra tarp or rain fly to secure over the front. (Another suggestion at the end of this article may be useful.)

Warmth: A teepee fire is the simplest to set up. Now how to make more efficient use of that heat... Build your fire pit FIRST and set up stones around it. (These should NOT be taken from a lake as they stand a good chance of exploding when heated.) Non-porous rock is what you want. Chances are if someone else has used rocks for their own campfires, you're reasonably safe. Set up 2 stakes on the side of the fire opposite your tent (about a metre high) and then roll aluminum foil sheets between the 2 stakes to form a fire reflector. If it's windy, you may have to use duct tape to hold the foil in place. Use the shiny side towards the fire. This will help reflect some of the fire's heat back towards you. Of course, DON'T leave it burning near the tent when you bed down.

Cooking: *Please refer to my Improv Cooking article. Lots of improv stove ideas.

Furnishings: (My, aren't we getting posh?) A cut section of a log can serve as a seat or a table. Here's an idea for people who just HAVE to have a picnic table. Make 4 tripods about 1/2m in length with sticks and lash them together. Set up the 4 tripods and then place 2 longer sticks to run parallel to each other. Then make a "ladder" using smaller sticks running across the 2 longer sticks. I've made a bed in this way as well as a rustic bench.

Now for the amenities- a wash basin set up on a log cut level along with a water jug, soap, towel, washcloth, etc.- all the comforts of a hotel. <u>Note</u>: Room Service won't be in to change your sheets, soap bar, or towels tomorrow morning. Harsh reality- you have to do that yourself.

In a pinch… you can turn a canoe over and prop it up on an angle with 2 "Y" sticks. The hull of the canoe would be facing the wind and rain affording you some protection. At night use the mattress and pillow, fire-reflector, ground tarp and mosquito netting. You may even secure the canoe totally upside down as an emergency shelter. Alternative: Turn the canoe right over and prop it up if the rain's coming straight down.

One final idea is to use a third tarp and run it over the front guyline of the tent in the event of rain. It would act as an "awning" over the front entrance. Fold it over the front guyline, spread it out and peg it down.

So here we have it: the rugged outdoors individual/cheapskate. It may be someone who has to improvise (which is <u>really</u> what this article is all about). The materials? Maybe 25-50m of rope, 2-3 tarps (small, larger and larger), 16-20 tent pegs, some old discarded drape sheers, a can for fire, a garbage bag and plastic shopping bag, blanket, sleeping bag, a roll of aluminum foil, maybe some duct tape and your imagination. An Improv Camp. More on other tarp shelters in a future article (Tarp Lean-to, teepee, sun shade). Please, <u>keep safe</u> and <u>have fun</u> outdoors. Remember that these ideas aren't fool-proof 100% or your money back ideas. They're meant to give you some tools and skills to use when you may need to make a situation better and safer. There are so many more techniques than we can discuss in the space of just one article. Use your imagination, creativity and ingenuity. Plan for the unexpected. Have a strategy or 2 up your sleeve and some spare equipment. Next month is a surprise. Bye for now.

Outdoors Guy

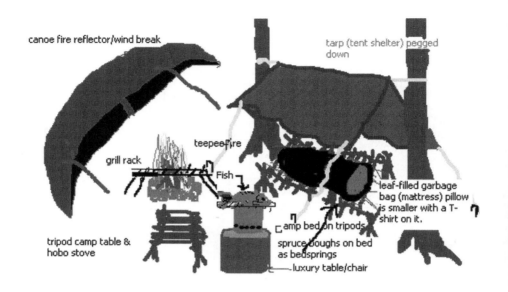

canoe fire reflector/wind break

tarp (tent shelter) pegged down

teepee fire

grill rack

Fish

leaf-filled garbage bag (mattress) pillow is smaller with a T-shirt on it.

tripod camp table & hobo stove

camp bed on tripods

spruce boughs on bed as bedsprings

luxury table/chair

The Noble Art of Scavenging

I'm going to say it straight up. This article is disgusting. It's the off season and I've been looking for an excuse to write this. I'll give you a hint...I didn't pay a single penny. Reactions to this may range from disgust to skepticism about the writer being in his right mind to amusement. It's all OK with me. I have another purpose in mind other than being cheap (and I've had to use it). That is that a survivor has to improvise with what their surroundings have to offer. Eating insects isn't on the menu until there's literally nothing around. There may also be a possibility that you just "forgot to pack that". A tent, fishing rod, bug spray, camp chair. No worries. Wait and see how the list of basic necessities is filled one by one. Outdoors Guy has got you covered! (*I also present a challenge... What is the one item I haven't found yet- besides a tent? I have everything else in the scenario, but I'm stuck without one of these.)

In my travels I have found the following items (in paragraph form to save space). Rope, 2 tarps, 2 windbreakers, 3 camp chairs, a driver, golf balls, other golf clubs, 3 golf bags, numerous lighters, a Gap™ sweatshirt, 2 paddles, 3 life jackets, 2 pairs of clean, pressed, tailored shorts, an emergency survival kit with tea, coffee, a hexamine stove, first aid pouch, space blanket, CO detector, power bars, etc., all the terminal tackle I need for the next 3 years for salmon and trout fishing, a whole box of salmon spoons and a few regular spoons, flashlights (1 really good one!), t shirts, blankets, a sleeping bag (*CLEAN!!!), a stand up grill rack and other grill racks, a bag of kindling and a bag of fire logs, a bag of briquettes, Browning™ and Shimano™ spinning reels, a 9ft. rod, a spinning rod and reel (Shakespeare), a net, a Shimano™ ice fishing rod and reel, a kids spinning outfit, sunscreen, bug repellent, lures, pliers, camp candles (the 3 ft. ones), 2 folding bush knives, towels, money(always helps...), sealed beer, 2 coolers, a folding camp fry pan, paper towels, a backpack, binoculars, tote bags, 2 suitcases (a day apart from each other!), tent pegs, 2 rain suits, soap, a TV with built in DVD player, sunglasses, reading glasses, a fry pan, a baking pan, a pot, and 2 umbrellas, garbage bags, matches, toilet paper, dish soap, scouring pads, tongs for grilling, coffee cans, skewers, a tea cup, a toy rake, clothes pegs, cooking utensils and 16 dried side dishes. You may be thinking-everything but the kitchen sink. Get ready for this... This year I found a kitchen sink. Hard to lug around camping so I passed up on it. Sigh…

Now add to this 3 garage sales… a moving sale in my complex got me lures and a lure box ($5), a portable camp shower and a water jug (all brand new), another complex sale got me a bait casting rod and reel and a spinning rod and reel (Shimano™, Abu Garcia/Cardinal™, Daiwa™), and another garage sale got me a warm vest, and a floodlight that plugs into the cigarette lighter in my car. This summer I was given an anchor found in a shed. Can life get any better??? We took some drapes down in our house and I kept the sheers. A scavenger saves everything. But I had a purpose. Keep reading and you'll see.

Now put all this neat junk together. With the rope and tarps and pegs you can set up a shelter with a groundsheet and rake enough leaves for a garbage bag mattress. Place the drape sheers over the front to keep out bugs. You have a sleeping bag and blankets to snuggle into. You have the lighters, coals, kindling, and firewood to start a fire. You have the pot, pans, grill racks, and utensils to cook with. You can improvise with the coffee cans and charcoal to make a Hobo stove which will, incidentally, serve to warm you if the weather is chilly. You have the dish detergent and scouring pads to wash up after dinner. You have the life jacket, paddles, fishing rods and reels, net and lures to go catch dinner with and needle nose pliers to remove the lure from the fish. You have the knives to clean the catch and perform numerous other tasks. The flashlights and torch candles will light your camp at night. You have the bathroom essentials. You have the shower, tarp for a shower stall, soap, towels, for washing.

You have camp chairs for yourself and a couple of friends, a back pack for hiking or storage, and a few beers and a cooler. A few clothes to give you swank, a sweatshirt, windbreakers and vest in case it gets chilly or windy. A space blanket in case it gets really chilly. Rain suits for keeping dry. You have sunscreen and insect repellent to protect you from UV rays and bugs. Garbage bags can do numerous things, apart from the obvious. You have an emergency kit. The water jug will store enough to keep you hydrated. You can even play a round of mini golf. You can string up a clothesline and hang out the unmentionables.

Yes, I am a scavenger! I feel that this noble art is somehow being lost in our advanced society. So really, I'm doing the environment a favour, and I'm returning to something more primitive and visceral in human nature- the vestige of the real person, the instinct for survival. And let's not forget that, deep down, if we'll be honest with ourselves, there's a bit of a cheapskate in every one of us- something that is thrilled to get something for nothing- the "bargain hunter par excellence". This person may be of the low down, shifty type, but I believe they are in some way part of the true human spirit. We are born to survive hardship, to fight, to persevere in the face of adversity, to seize opportunity… OK, I'll stop.

All kidding aside, what if you were stranded and HAD NO CHOICE but to depend on anything and everything you could find to survive. This instinct would quickly trump every other instinct. Nobody's going to argue about you getting it free in this situation. In fact- you're the HERO! Who cares if there's nowhere to plug in the TV/DVD player? You, being the true survivor can find your own fun. There's also the bright side. No taxes on the land, no energy bills, fresh air, no traffic, no noise, no concrete, no nerve shredding fast-paced schedules or deadlines… We humans were BORN for this! I'm so excited I'm tempted to drive 500 miles North and stay there. Come back (maybe) in 20 years in overalls and a beard that would make Duck Dynasty™ jealous.

I had so much fun writing this. I admit, I'm an incurable scavenger, and PROUD OF IT! But think about the benefits. A little bush craft and all this heady stuff and you've got the complete campsite. The missing item? A canoe. My son trumped me when someone just literally left a tent beside his site after a rock concert! I still want that canoe! (An excuse to keep scavenging.) After all, we all thrive on a challenge.

Your Pal,

Outdoors Guy

"Honey, Let's Get Some Furniture" ("OK, you asked for it...")

This is a reasonable request. C'mon guys… You HONESTLY expect to live in a makeshift shelter at a campsite and cheap out on furniture? What kind of skinflint are you? People deserve a little comfort- some amenities. "Hey, it ain't much, but it's home." You may be able to sell this notion better with some furnishings. Get your camp saw, axe, lashing and maybe a few spiral nails ready and let's make this dump, I mean campsite, homey.

I'm going back to my 2 recent articles on "The Totally Improv Camp" and the "Noble Art of Scavenging". This article tags along. We discussed Fire in a recent article. Fire makes things cozy- does so much. Let's add more to the camp ambience and furnish.

Have I done these things? Yes, I have. And it was FUN!! Mind, you, I was only looking for furniture for myself- one of those "Bachelor Apartment" things.

The basic foundation for your furnishings is a simple tripod. Cut 3 12" - 15" sticks of inch thick fresh hardwood. Lash the sticks together at one end forming a tripod with the lashing about 3 inches from the top. Open up the top and spread the base into an equilateral triangle. Create 4 of these.

Now first... the bed. Use 4 tripods and then find some STURDY heavier braches about 2" in diameter to form the bedrails. Lay them lengthwise along the long sides of the frame. Next, find as many "slats" as possible from sticks which aren't decayed and brittle. Lay as many of these as you can across the 2 longer poles. Be careful of slats that are crooked and stick out. As smooth and straight as possible is what you want. Your bed is now ready. (*As much as I hate to say it, twin beds are the order here. A double-sized bed is harder to support. Sorry Dear!) I had several adults and a 10 year old girl try my tripod bed. They all liked it thought it was comfy.

Now for the luxury and comfort- Lay as many spruce and pine branches over top of the frame as possible- the thicker the layering, the more comfortable the bed. Top with dry leaves- as high as practical. The leaves will compress so you want lots of padding.

Voila...1 bed! You can now make a shade for it by running a guy line between 2 trees. Place a tarp over the guy line over your bed and secure it with shorter ropes and pegs. You now have a sun-shade which may also help if it starts raining lightly. (*See: "What You Can Do With a Tarp")

Next- a bench or chairs to sit on- same idea. 4 tripods, 2 longer, stronger support beams and some crossbars. I also have used 2 grill racks over my support beams as my seat, covered with pine boughs- totally luxurious.

If you are fortunate enough to find some pre-cut logs from a thick tree trunk, you have seats and possibly a table. These will also serve very handily for a wash station. Just rest your wash basin on one log and water jug on another, slightly longer one.

By now you may be thinking, "When do we install the shower? Bingo! You can buy a shower bag with a shower head that hangs from a tree. It holds 2 gallons of water, is black, and heats merely by placing it in the sun. For privacy, string a tarp around 3 trees close together to form an enclosure. Just run the rope thru the grommets in the tarp and string up your shower curtain to the desired height. Use the line later as a clothes line. Just hand the shower bag on a tree branch overhead and let the warm water flow. Tip… to make sure you've got enough rinse water, get wet, shut the tap off, soap up, then loosen the tap again to rinse off. ("Navy" Shower)

But, Honey, we need a washing machine! I agree! Take a 5 gallon, CLEAN pail with a lid. (Ideal pails are ones used by custodians which have a pouring spout in the lid.) Cut the spout off or cut a hole in the lid large enough to allow a broom handle to slide thru easily. Here's the trick. Now get a NEW (**NOT USED!!**) plunger. This is the "agitator" for your new washing machine. Use the solar shower water for hot water washing. Just place the clothes in the machine with soap and water and agitate. If the pioneers can churn butter, you can agitate. Clothes line ready as mentioned before. If there's a disagreement over this modern convenience, it may help to point out some alternatives…washboard, pounding clothes on a rock…etc.

We need a fridge!! (Oh, what next??) I've seen this but haven't tried it yet. The Clay Pot Cooler. Take 2 earthen plant pots- 1 slightly larger than the other. Cover the bottom hole of the base pot (the larger one) with duct tape. Place a layer of sand on the bottom of the pot, then place the smaller pot in the larger one- right in the middle. Fill in the space between the 2 pots with clean sand. Now moisten the layer of sand with cool water. Place a few cold ones in the pot, and cover with a wet, clean towel. Place in the shade and wait a few hours. I've seen this work on-line. The bottles were frosty. I haven't done this myself, but it was impressive. Worth a try- remember, you can always take this appliance back...

What next for our dream home/love nest- a table? Same deal using the tripods. IF you can find a large flat piece of wood, say about an inch to 2 inches thick, what a table top! Nail it down to a log centre piece or use 3 or 4 logs as table legs.

You can make a really good space for storage by lashing together a tepee of 4 long sticks- about 5 ft. each. Make a square out of sticks, lash together, and place it over the frame so that it rests about 2 ft. from the ground. Lay cross pieces over the square and presto, a shelf. You can then use a smaller square for a smaller shelf 2 feet higher up. (*See diagram.)

OK. Beds, showers, shower stalls, shade, washing machine, drying, chairs/benches, a table, wash stand (vanity of vanities), a...STOVE!

Since I've mentioned a host of camp "stoves" and heaters, I won't repeat. Please refer to the articles on "Improv Cooking" and "What You Can Do With a Can" for an improv meat smoker.

Washing up. A good tip is to cover the bottom of pots and pans with soap. The best scouring pads I've ever seen are the centers from buffer pads, used by janitors on floors. Failing that, ball up some old fishing line and use it as a scouring pad. The soap will make clean up easier. Use the old wash water to extinguish a cooking fire.

Furnace? A fire pit and Hobo Heater. Simple enough. A reflector wall will help re-radiate heat, something like a crude type of wall insulation. (*See Wood Shelters Article in Survival Section.)

With some woodcraft you can fashion a welcome sign (or, more appropriately, "Go Home", "No Trespassing"…)

You can cut out steak plates from slices of logs. You can make a photo booklet with string and 2 pieces of thin wood as book covers. Or use birch bark for that rustic antique look. Make a picture frame for Aunt Martha or Uncle Willard or a pine cone wreath for Christmas. A few small braches lashed around a larger stick at the bottom can serve for a rake and broom so you can do the house and yard work.

Almost forgot the most important thing- A toilet? Use a 5 gallon pail with a potty seat or even a seat cut out from a plank of wood. This should be DOWNWIND for obvious reasons. Waste disposal should be FAR from any place where water can be contaminated and buried. (*This is useful if you don't want to trek to the outhouse- you can just "deposit" in the outhouse next morning.). Plus…BUY toilet paper. You can't compromise on EVERYTHING, you know. Practicality trumps pioneer spirit here. I should also mention soap. It is possible to create a very crude soap using ashes, water and fat. DON'T! This is very harsh. Buy soap.

There is a definite advantage to all this. No marital conflict over spending more than you can afford, especially if you're just starting out. Nosey neighbours? Choose a site a healthy distance from local busy-bodies.

Finally, that candle light dinner... Buy some 3 ft. citronella camp candles from the dollar store. They furnish the cheapest camp lighting available and burn for several hours. Ah...the ambience, the modern inconveniences, the ingenuity, the paper plates and plastic utensils and cups, the endless patience of your partner trying to put up with all this. Wishing you HAD a partner to put up with all this... It may just well be, however, that you've found your true soul mate and that this arrangement suits you both just fine. No phone, no lights, no motorcar... Not a single luxury?? Oh reeeeaaaalllly?? And who **CARES** about "Keeping up with the Joneses?" or, "What will the neighbours think?" If you're looking for a starter house and starter sets of things, look no further! It beats buying the cheap stuff on credit! "It ain't much, but it's paid for." How many of us can make <u>that </u>claim? J

Yours in Jest, (...but I also hope for some good ideas for DIY camp furnishings too!)

SWAMP BED

Make 4 of these

One of the best things about this set-up is you can acrry the 4 tripods with you to your next campsite.

Lay the tripods out evenly at 4 corners. Spread them out so they balance and open wide. Lay 2 long-strong, thicker sticks as the mainframe. Cross with slightly smaller sticks. Test it! Don't use sticks that are flimsy/rotted.

1 /12 inches thick and young, strong wood. Lash securely.

This same set-up can be used to construct a camp chair/bench or table. Be careful if it's a bed. The sticks should be smooth and striaght or they dig into you when you're lying on them. You can now layer these with pine/spruce boughs, leaves/garbage bag mattress.

Your Storage Unit. Lash together 4 upright poles and spread them out. Lash together a larger square of 4 stciks and lay this over the frame (lower shelf). Repeat with a smaller square higher up (upper shelf). Lay sticks along the squares as cross pieces. Voila!

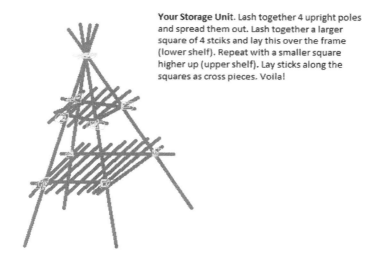

Handling a Canoe

One of the most useful outdoors life skills that will last a life-time is learning how to handle a canoe. There are a few basic principles of stability that apply to maintaining the safe position of a canoe. The first principle is Low Centre of Gravity. Standing up raises your centre of gravity which causes the canoe to become unstable. You want to keep as LOW as possible in a seated or kneeling posture while still being comfortable.

The second principle is like unto the first: Weight should be centred in the middle of the canoe from left to right. You'll soon feel and see the canoe shift if you don't sit squarely in the middle.

Third principle: Weight of what is loaded into a canoe is evenly distributed. Now here's a tip with this thought in mind. If you are trying to paddle the canoe quickly to avoid, let's say, being out in wind and rain, it's a good idea to stabilize the bow (front) of the canoe with some weight to keep the nose in the water. Otherwise the canoe may "plane" on you with the bow raised by your weight in the back. To steer an even course, it helps to have the stern (front) in the water.

Getting into a canoe: I was taught this way: Reach over the middle bar in the canoe or reach for the further gunwale (edge) with your lead hand. Staying LOW, step in with your lead foot and grasp the other (closer) gunwale with your other hand. You now have control of the canoe's position with both hands. Carefully step into the canoe with your other foot and settle yourself into the middle comfortably.

Safety: Best to have your life jacket on before getting in the canoe. Just like fastening your seat belt before starting your car.

We'll look at three basic strokes for handling, propelling and directing a canoe: the Draw Stroke, The Sweep Stroke, and The "J" Stroke.

The Draw Stroke: Very simple and useful to draw your canoe along-side a dock parallel. Simply dip the blade of the canoe into the water and "pull it towards you". This moves the canoe a relatively small distance and is used to reach a dock when you're already in close.

The Sweep Stroke: This is a power stroke. You simply paddle with the blade mostly submerged on one side of the boat. This propels the boat forward IN THE OPPOSITE DIRECTION. (Example: A Sweep Stroke on the right side of the canoe will move you LEFT.) This may be very useful if you battling a breeze that's pushing your canoe to one side, meaning that you have to propel the canoe against it in order to maintain course.

The "J" Stroke: This stroke is intended to allow you to paddle on one side of a canoe and maintain a straight course. It can be tiring on your shoulder because of the turning you have to do with your paddle. Picture yourself above a canoe watching a person paddle. They start with a sweep stroke then move the paddle out and around a bit so the blade of the paddle draws a letter "J" on the water. This gives you propulsion and direction. To save stress on your shoulder, turn the paddle with your hands, try not to push the paddle into a "j" using only your arms. Relax and switch to a sweep stroke at regular intervals to give your muscles a break.

BTW…If you need to turn the canoe around in a small space, simply do a sweep stroke backwards.

Tandem paddling allows you to gain the most momentum. 2 canoeists sweep-stroking. A sweep stroke gives you the most forward momentum.

I was trained in righting, emptying, and re-entering a canoe but it's better to get real hands on training for yourself rather than just trying it with no practice. If you're WEARING A LIFE JACKET (Hint, Hint…) kick to the surface turn the canoe over. On top of the water and empty, it can be flipped over. If the canoe is too long and large for you to attempt this as one person, try to roll it over in as high a position as possible to at least get it to float upright. I was taught to re-enter a canoe by grasping the gunwale opposite to the side I was on, spreading my weight across the top, and then kicking forward and pulling myself in. It is likely there'll be a fair amount of water in the canoe so you'll have to do a lot of bailing. If you've been able to roll the canoe and elevate it to some degree, you are likely to be able to keep afloat in it well enough to bail it out. The idea here is definitely to stay in the MIDDLE! Remember, the canoe is nearly full- you don't want to tip it and end up back in the drink again- having to try and repeat the whole process. It worked, but again, please get some proper hands-on training. The easiest thing to do is simply to swim with the canoe if you're close to shore, get out of the water, and then climb in again. If you have floating gear and the canoe is upright, you can use the weight of the gear to stabilize the canoe if you try and re-enter it. Remember the principle: LOW centre of gravity- weight distributed LOW as possible. Priorities are priorities. SAVE YOUR LIFE FIRST. You can buy more gear later.

Tip: <u>Always</u> carry a spare paddle. If your paddle slips out of your hands all you've got left are your hands to paddle with. In a pinch, use the life preserver to paddle. You may also wish to carry a spare life jacket. You can use it to assist in signaling if the canoe has gone down. It would also be helpful to carry a floating kneeling pad. It makes kneeling more comfortable, and it may save your life if you've got nothing else to assist you in keeping afloat. You also should have a bailing bucket. (*See Art of Improv I for a suggestion- the bleach/detergent bottle.) Even a child's plastic sand bucket can do the job. I used 2 pool noodles to replace the bumper pads on my canoe this summer. They add buoyancy. Consider, maybe, using foam bumper pads to help keep your canoe on top if it flips. Everything helps.

Are waves rising? Get OFF the water if the wind and waves are picking up. I've found that it's safer to angle a canoe into (perpendicular to) waves. Sitting parallel to waves (say they were created by a passing powerboat) makes the canoe rock and roll. If you feel you have to steady the canoe before you can turn perpendicular to the waves, grip the gunwales on both sides and get lower. If you see lightning, GET TO SHORE IMMEDIATELY!

As usual- put safety first. The smaller the craft, the more respect needed for wind and waves. A small craft may be easier to turn upright again, but it may also be more unstable as winds pick up. I would like to be able to offer guarantees with this article. Perhaps, more than with any other article and subject, this is the one where I have state that what I've said is never 100% foolproof. Water safety has to be taught, learned, and practiced BEFORE you have to use emergency measures. At the risk of sounding redundant, PLEASE take a canoeing and water safety course. PRACTICE in controlled circumstances WITH AN INSTRUCTOR AND WITH A LIFE JACKET ON until you KNOW you can handle an over-turned canoe. This could be a matter of survive or not (said very carefully). Conditioning plays a role here. KNOWLEDGE and PRACTICE play a role here- having floatation devices which are approved and in new condition plays a role here. Having extra equipment like a kneeling mat, second PFD, a whistle, something brightly coloured and/or shiny to signal for help with all raise your chances. Give yourself every advantage possible. This isn't the time to assume, "Yah, I'd know what to do." People who say this sound a warning note in my head. I was stuck recently with a flat tire in the pouring rain- in the winter and at night having to try and figure everything out from the manual. No success. Of course I had to call the CAA. Righting an over-turned canoe is a similar such instance except that you are in the water and the "manual" has sunk to the bottom. Moral: The time to start learning what to do is NOT when something happens.

Canoes can take people into unimaginable places. They were likely the first means of water travel in North America. Being safe means returning home to tell stories and show photo-graphs. I know I've said it before…but…PLEASE BE SAFE- Make Equipment and Training Priority #1.

Outdoors Guy

Outdoors Guy- Storing Wars

I hope you've had a nice summer. It'll be time soon to store all that gear for the winter. The time to prepare for another happy trip next year is now.

Here are some common things to do and not do.

Tents should be thoroughly swept and wiped down. Any sand or mud on the floor should be washed off and the tent completely dried. DON'T store the tent in the shed outside. Find a clean, dry place away from paint and gasoline fumes. Here's the basic idea for my sermon...the way you pack it away is the way you'll open it up next time. Your tent is your shelter. Take the time and do things properly. If it's been raining, allow time for the tent to dry- completely. Brush all the dirt off the rings at the corners and remove dirt from the ends of the tent poles so that they'll fit next year. Note any seams that have been leaking and seal them with a water repellent. Allow the water repellant solvent time to vapourize into the air so you don't have fumes next year. Do the same thing with the ground tarp you use under your tent. Sweep, wash down, dry, fold and then store.

Part of my outdoor learning has come from my mistakes... I left my biker's tent in the shed one winter. When I went up camping the next year, I unrolled the tent to find a nice 2 ft. square hole where the material had rotted. It accommodated the mosquitoes perfectly. So clean, dry, stored in a cool dry place is the idea. By the way, there are few things as irritating as having a tent returned, rolled up (you can see where this is going, can't you?), with grass and dirt all over the inside. You were nice enough, after all, to loan the tent to someone, then they return it in a mess. Give 'em the 3rd degree on this one.

Sleeping bags should be washed and dried, aired out, at least shaken and then aired out for next year. They must be absolutely dry or the material will develop mold.

Buy the flashlight and lantern batteries now and store them. What you do now allows you to avoid that trip into town next year.

Use up camp stove and lantern fuel now. Store your equipment in a dry place. It is safer with the tanks empty and you'll avoid problems with condensation. Clean the stove of any grease and rust. Storing in a dry place also helps prevent rust from forming over the winter.

Now the high tip... The best way I've found to store and pack is going modular. Devise your own system based on the style of camping you do. You can get this pretty efficient if you are a single camper and use "the basics". (My style- I have a small SUV and I have to have things well organized space-wise and weight-wise.) Make a game out of it- your own version of Storage Wars. Start with the categories- shelter, bedding, cooking gear, cooler (an important item at the end of a days' fishing as you can imagine), survival gear and camping accessories. Take a look at the space in your vehicle. I store my pot, pan, grill rack, utensils, spices, filleting knife, cutting board, newspaper, plastic/paper dishes & cutlery etc. in one bin. Wash the dishes when you get home and store- ready for next year.

My bedding is stored in a duffle bag. Got it for $4.00! It holds a blanket, camp pillow, sleeping mat, sleeping bag and a few spare items depending on the season.

My equipment bin holds my butane stove, lantern (battery-powered), tarps, a small shovel, rake, first-aid kit (Get a GOOD one! Don't cheap out on this!!), matches, Do It Yourself fire start-ers (dryer lint handily stored in toilet paper rolls- ready to use as tinder to start the next campfire), aluminum foil (start the sea-son with a new roll), and accessories such as fish-stringer, drape sheers in case on a rip in the mosquito netting, tool kit, duct tape, hammer, multi-tool. Take the time to think of the eternal equation- Great Camping = Necessary Items /Available Space. What do you have to make sure you bring with you? Referring back to my previous article on survival basics, think of- Warmth/Dryness, Shelter, Tools, Water, Food, First Aid, Protection from the sun, insects, cold, wind, rain.

Now add to the equation some furniture like a camp chair and some fun stuff like fishing and hiking gear. So what do you pack to meet all these needs? It may be as individual as each person but it can be fun to actually sit down and think about it and play with it a bit. Once you've got it figured out (Don't worry-it'll always change a bit for each trip- that's half the fun.), you can start sorting what goes into each bin. It makes packing far quicker. And when you store your equipment, you don't have to re-think the whole process next year. You've got the bases covered. Your equipment is clean, dry in good condition and ready for use again.

I have all my survival and emergency gear in one backpack. Note the use of a backpack- you may have to travel on foot if you run into an emergency.

Booster cables and plug in flood light are under the passenger seat.

MAXIM: "Take good care of your equipment and it'll take good care of you." No comment needed, really.

FINAL NOTE: Seriously, preparation ahead of time is EVERYTHING. Imagine how good it feels to have everything you need organized, in good working order, ready to unpack for the next camping season. You've got all the bases covered. My advice toward this goal: make an extensive list and check it off every time before you leave for an excursion. For a laugh, imagine the joy of unpacking a rotted tent or groundsheet, moldy sleeping bag, having dead batteries, greasy cooking implements, out of this, forgot that...This separates us into 2 distinct "parties"- "The Haven't Got a Clue Party" Or...The "I'm Going to Have a Party." This Party prepares, organizes, plans...and ends up saving themselves multiple annoyances- and has more fun. They also save money on their equipment because they take care of it. They ensure that they have what they need and it works. They pack and store with a plan. Leave the first campers at home or let them camp by themselves. They can get wet, be left in the dark, run out of bug spray...etc. Hey, we all have to learn by our experiences. Storing smart can go hand in hand with packing smart. You arrive at your destination with everything you need and working for you the way it was designed to. Then you can have fun.

Till Next Time. Your Pal,

Outdoors Guy

Summer Vacations

"Get 'em out of the house. Go to the mountains, go to the beach, go anywhere, but GO! Or you'll go nuts." (Quote: Professor Ludwig Von Drake on what to do with the kids during Summer Vacation.)

So true. We have instant entertainment like never before with smart phones, tablets, portable DVD Players. So, yes, the kids can bring all the entertainment they want- as long as they can keep their devices charged. Having said that, I really believe that there's something inside that'll still love the outdoors and new things to try.

We always planned well ahead for our Summer camp trips. This was between 25 and 12 years ago so no smart phones or tablets yet. The lists seemed endless- food menus, snacks, daily activities, clothes, bedding, fresh food in the cooler, toys... They were fun times. Our children did have hand held games then, but they were really good sports. They were happy to spend a week doing outdoor things. What follows are some of the activities and planning tips we used back in the day. Mom was a planning and preparing Trooper and Saint.

I designed a 9-hole mini golf course one year, complete with score cords. Everyone got a practice golf ball and club and we played for a prize.

Hiking: We walked the trails. When the kids were old enough, they walked themselves. This became part (this is important) of our family "traditions". A tradition is something established so we have to do it every year. Traditions become something your children always look back and have good memories about. And they are important because it's your own special "thing" that you're family shares. Make fun things a part of your traditions.

First Nations Day: (And I say this with great respect.) Mom wasn't feeling well one day and had to rest. I caught on to the idea of using fallen birch bark to create tipis, canoes, etc. We made fish drying racks with twigs and toothpicks. Then we made masks using paper plates. We topped it all off by roasting hot dogs and having canned peaches and donuts for dessert. They loved it so...you can guess...we did this every year and it became part of our family...tradition.

We were fortunate to have a pioneer schoolhouse right on the property at our campsite. So every year involved a trip to see how the other side learned years ago. It became a (repeat after me....) family tradition. Why not make it a part of the whole package to visit a local landmark or museum? You only have to see it once. The beauty of web searches is that finding a new place to explore next year should be easy.

Pack Plenty of Comics. They just got passed around.

Bring a friend or 2. Invite another family to come up as guests-for a day or 2.

Get the kids involved in planning meals! Nothing has to be a big production. Hot dogs and grilled cheese, macaroni and cheese, soup, fruit, roasted marshmallows and S'mores aren't hard to make. They always did a great job. The point is, they're getting involved! THEY have ownership over a project.

Use the time to begin to teach children outdoor skills. This ISN'T a lost art! Every life skill enriches their lives. Simple things like how to use a compass, how to build a lean-to, how to navigate by the sun, moon, and stars, how to rig up a makeshift tent, cook over a fire using a grill, tripod, or spit, how to recognize footprints. Have the kids even plan a day outing as they begin to accumulate outdoor skills. An overnight excursion would be the ultimate but choose a safe place close to main camp.

Use the occasion to tell stories passed on by our First Nations friends.

Have the kids bring some costumes and create some skits.

Bring books and puzzle books you've been saving and haven't told them about.

A water fight NEVER loses its appeal. Bring the squirt guns or balloons.

Have a frog race. (Return the frogs to nature.)

Bring paints and plenty of paper so they can capture their surroundings.

A couple of board games may be well placed. Even "Poker Night". Keep the bets friendly…

Arts and Crafts are a MUST! Along with paints, they can create picture frames, book designs, signs, beaded jewelry, dream catchers, etc. They have a treasure to bring home. The bracelet and beading kits are still popular with the girls.

Play license plate cribbage on the way up to the camp or cottage. Have a board to keep score.

Break the trip up into parts. Pull in at a rest stop, have a bathroom break, eat, and stretch. It is monotonous for children to sit for one long stretch in the car.

Everyone has their assigned chores to do. This doesn't sound like fun but routine is your friend. Co-operation and shared responsibility are good life skills. Build a sense of TEAMWORK.

Make use of shared activities with other campers (beach volleyball, baseball, horseshoes, etc.)

Visit a Mini Putt.

Connect with friends and/or family close by for a yearly drop in.

Have some new beach toys (safe ones!!!). A beach can be a whole afternoon's entertainment. Sand castles are still "in".

Play a family trivia game. Ask questions about previous trips, books they've read, movies they've watched, places they've visited.

Have lots of snacks for break time.

Start with a plan for the day and be ready to vary it. If the kids get "onto something", stay at it.

Scavenger hunts are a BLAST. You want to be careful not to send the kids into tall grasses where rattlesnakes are known to frequent. The key is to keep them in sight and use the older siblings to help supervise. Get them to look for simple items and sometimes give them a criterion instead of an item. Example: Find something you can use to create a dream catcher. No toads-they can give off a toxic secretion on their skins.

Plan a Treasure Hunt with clues- one adult/older sibling per group.

Plan one night into town to a restaurant and/or movie.

Teach the kids basic canoeing skills- the sweep, draw and "J" strokes. When they get a bit older they can play war canoes by following each other around and throwing wet sponges at the "enemy". Besides, canoeing is a great life outdoor skill.

Teach the kids to mark trails and practice signaling. This may come in handy in later life if they find themselves in an emergency and have to call for help.

Ask the kids what they'd do if they were out in the woods and were challenged with creating a makeshift camp. Bring some supplies like a tarp, rope, tent pegs, blankets, etc. with you and see what they can create.

Make sure that the kids understand basic fire making and extinguishing principles. Use dry rocks from a previous fire pit. Teach them how to gather tinder, kindling, and fuel and how to at least construct a tipi and stacked log/cross-hatched fire.

We used to collect wildflowers for a bouquet for Mom. *With respect to the environment, why not take photos and arrange them in a collage?

Build an inuksuk. Careful with this one. I'd advise staying away from boulders for rather obvious reasons- the flatter the rocks the better. Place your inuksuk in a more or less permanent spot and take photos to hang up at home. Watch climbing onto higher, dangerous, harder to reach spots. This doesn't have to be a crash course in mountain climbing.

Use your outdoors time to teach and practice first aid and safety- water safety, fire safety, keeping food out of reach of predatory animals, camp routines for keeping things tidy and organized. Have the kids practice first aid in simulated situations. It all comes back to them later, really. They may be grateful that they learned what to do when they were younger.

If the kids come up with a fun idea, and it's safe, why not let 'em try it? They are famous for their imagination. Talk about an idea and shape it so it is safe and maybe add a few embellishments to it.

Take some down time from activity. It doesn't have to be go, go, go constantly. A change of pace is as important a part of the whole day as is the next activity. I never said don't bring smart phones and games and tablets and portable DVD Players- allot a specific time for them. Evenings after a day of shared activities are a good time. Everyone needs their own personal time and space, whether at home or on vacation. You aren't banning them, you are using them as a part of the total venue. Getting away means just being able to add other, new things to their life experiences. Besides, there ARE those hours in the car...

Collect and print the photos and place each summer's collection in a scrapbook. The kids design the cover.

*I'd like to say that preparation and planning and research are the most important parts of a trip- by FAR! Let the kids know a lot of what you've planned so you're not just hitting them with what seems like an iron-clad agenda. Have family meetings and talk about what they really enjoyed and what was ho-hum. Don't give up if one idea doesn't seem to go down well. Ask them what THEY'D suggest. Find out ahead of time some of the things THEY'D like to do and learn more about. Plan something special to each child. It's SO much work, but worth every moment of it! Finally, be informed and knowledgeable YOURSELF first. Do your OWN HOMEWORK. Find out places of interest. Research the trails. Know first aid and camp/woods craft. Know safety precautions and follow them routinely.

Summer vacations are a priceless time- a strange sort of paradox- the more you work at it, the more you play and relax and enjoy it. HAVE FUN!!!!! You have been given a great opportunity, make the most of it. One of the greatest lessons we'll ever learn is how to have fun. Children begin their lives with play, adults have to re-learn it. Do BOTH in the summer.

Outdoors Guy

The Fourth Element

The ancient wisdom of our forebears postulated that there were 4 elements: earth, air, water, and fire. In keeping with this thesis and in view of the fact that it's getting cold outside, this article is devoted to one of the critical elements of survival in the outdoors- fire.

Fire can cook your food for you, boil water to purify it, provide light, warmth, protection, send out a signal to potential rescuers, and, in a curious way, create a sense of comfort and familiarity in your campsite. As the hero Aragorn, in *The Lord of the Rings* trilogy said, "…fire is our friend in the wilderness."

Three basic elements are necessary for creating fire. I'm going to take a writer's liberty here and say, without specifying, that there's also a <u>Fourth Element</u>- the Fourth Element of the Fourth Element if you will. I'm having some fun with this and would like to ask you to think about it. Let's begin with…

Tinder: This is where you start. The lightest, fluffiest, <u>driest</u> materials you can find. Atop my list is dryer lint. I bring it with me when camping so I don't have to go searching for every fire. Packed in individual toilet paper rolls and then into a coffee can, this takes up minimal space and I'm good for 6-10 fires. Other excellent tinder includes: dry pine needles (loaded with turpentine), birch bark, which in my opinion goes up better and faster than even newspaper (please don't strip living trees if you don't have to), balled up masking or duct tape, black tree fungus, and any kind of fluff from long grasses, so long as it's dry. Cattail fluff from the brown tops of bull rushes is excellent. The tinder should be arranged in a dry space under your kindling, and loosely packed to allow for air. If you can find a spruce tree with lots of "bumps" in the bark, these are pockets of resin. This resin burns very well and can help maintain a flame a bit longer. You can even use it for a pine cone torch if you can collect enough. Now for the...

Kindling: This consists of small twigs ranging to thin sticks. To harp on the obvious- they must be DRY. There are 2 basic types of campfires I like to use which are relatively easy to set up if you have the right materials, and which quickly produce a hot fire that, if managed properly, can be sustained and controlled.

Type 1 is the tepee fire. Stack twigs and small sticks into a tepee formation. The slant of the sticks produces an updraft which produces a hot fire and which can quickly accept larger pieces of wood.

Type 2 was taught to me many years ago by a First Nations teen my wife and I met at a Provincial Park. This is called a stacked log or cross-hatched fire. Small pieces of kindling wood are arranged- let's say 4 pieces going west to east then 4 more pieces going at 90° from north to south. You alternate the pieces of wood so that no one piece is directly over top of another piece to allow for maximum airflow. A clever variation on this idea is to build a log cabin type of structure with a layer of sticks over the "roof" to protect tinder and lower layers of kindling in case of a light rain. You can even build your "log cabin" over a tepee fire to protect it. So now we have created a small fire which needs to continually be fed so we add…

Fuel: Larger pieces of dried wood. Even here, there is some thinking involved. Soft woods like pine and spruce will burn faster than hardwoods. They can be added first to keep the momentum of the fire going. (From my experience softwood also creates more flying sparks than hardwood, so be careful.) However, they won't last long. Hardwoods burn much longer- great stuff for sitting around the camp fire and telling stories and opening a few cold ones.

Think and plan even in such a seemingly simple scenario as this. Place wood on an upward slant facing into the centre of the fire, or maintain the cross-hatch configuration so your new wood is constantly igniting well and producing high heat. Laying wood flat doesn't cut it (bad pun) because you're covering your coals.

If you pile all your wood on at once, you're wasting it. If you were on a survivor show, you'd deserve a dunking in the lake for this mistake. A piece or two to maintain the fire and keep warm will help conserve your wood supply far longer. If you WERE in a survival situation, you'd figure out pretty quickly that you couldn't afford to waste any of your precious fuel. Why waste it anyway?

A few of the books I've read stress collecting much more wood than you think you'll need, even for one night- absolutely correct. Your wood supply is one of the easiest things to under-estimate. So my rule is: collect 6 times more than you think you'll need. You'll see. It burns as fast as a monthly pay check- best to have plenty to spare.

Face it- wet wood won't burn, but...you can cheat a little. The underside of some logs may be dry so burn the dry side first. If you have softwood for kindling and it's damp on the outside from a little rain, use a hatchet and split the wood exposing the dry interior. If you are fortunate enough, most of the inside could still be dry and thus you can still ignite it.

Have a tarp or garbage bags to cover your wood complete-ly and weigh it/them down with small rocks. DON'T go to bed assuming, "Aw, it won't rain tonight!" Some people only learn thru experience... Personally, this careless camper can go camp somewhere else. (Say, in nice damp cave??)

ALWAYS have at least 3 sources for starting a fire. I'm not in love with the romanticism of rubbing two sticks together just for the sake of showing off my training. No thanks! I carry a dozen or 2 lighters and use them. Matches, magnifying glasses with larger lenses, flint and steel to spark an ember, and chemicals such as potassium permanganate and magnesium are all fire starters. Some work by producing a flame, some by producing a spark. Any commercially sold chemical product should be used with the label read and the directions followed SCRUPULOUSLY!

Fire must be contained and controlled. Like many other things, it is your friend if you're in control of it but can be a deadly enemy if allowed to run wild. Dig a fire pit at least 2 ½ to 3 feet in diameter. It should be dug down say 3-4 inches. The bottom can be covered with sand. The circumference of the pit should then be lined with rocks to contain the fire. **NOTE!!**: NEVER use rocks taking from a lake. They can expand and explode on you. (Liquids expand faster than solids and the rocks, if they're at all porous, contain water.) Use dry rocks from your surroundings. Granite is ideal.

Make sure your fire is a safe distance away from your tent. Sparks can fly in the wind and then your fire will be the only protection you have left. In addition, site selection is important. Near nearby leaf piles, dead softwoods with dried needles, etc. Have some thought ahead of time and choose your site with care. Remember, you want to CONTAIN and CONTROL your fire, especially in a windy situation- the stronger the wind, the lower the flame. If you are in an area with prevailing strong winds, consider digging your pit a little deeper.

We now come to it…The Fourth Element of the Fourth Element. It's ridiculously simple, yet can be overlooked. If… you…said…AIR- double Air Miles. GOOD!! My fire pit at one of my favourite camping spots is a good deep well lined pit. And that's the trouble! It is deep enough that my tinder and kindling don't always get enough oxygen. I have this personal belief that a properly constructed fire should only have to be lit ONCE. Believe it or not, this summer, I accomplished this very thing!! HOWEVER…I noticed that what I thought were properly constructed fires had trouble getting going. Dry tinder- check. Dry kindling arranged properly into the tipi or cross-hatch- check. Oh, yah, have to fan it! I took the lid off one of my Rubbermaid™ containers and fanned. What a difference! Some people may be thinking, "Isn't this OBVIOUS??" I admit it. So remember: "I'm a FAN of Fire!" (Don't fan sparks on your tent or in someone's face. There's such a thing as the overly-enthusiastic fan...)

On that note (my wife suggested this great addendum) if you have to make efficient use of your fire for warmth, consider constructing a fire reflector. I built one this spring using 3 upright poles and heavy duty aluminum foil. A stacked log wall is a common type of fire reflector. I have it on my bucket list for next year to see if a propped up canoe could also do the same task. I'll let you know. The Fire Reflector diagram is in the "Vital Heat Retention" article.

Lastly, to put out the fire completely (unless you have to survive in the cold- in which case you'll be staying up late to maintain it by feeding it little by little) use sand or water.

I know I haven't mentioned using friction methods to start a fire. So I'll be honest. I'm practicing- again next year's projects. The 3 methods I'll be practicing are a fire plough, hand drill, and bow drill. The scope of this article was really the components of fire. Friction methods are life-savers when there's nothing else left, but very work intensive. If I may ask your indulgence now and perhaps include them in a future article? I carry lots of lighters and match packs simply because, if you can make things easier, then do it. But, as I know some of you are thinking, you need to have a Plan B or C and know what to do- agreed- very worthwhile material for a future article.

Fire has attained an almost mystical status in some outdoor lore. I have sat by a fire and felt cheered up, warmed up- as though I'm not QUITE alone anymore- a feeling like being home, a bit safer and more protected. This year I tried tripod cooking, and grilling with a portable stand-up grill rack. Next year, God willing, spit cooking, and maybe even a Dutch Oven. That's what I LOVE about the outdoors- there's always something new out there.

Your Friend and Fellow Traveler,

Outdoors Guy

Tipi Fire: Black tinder fungus, dead birch bark, dried pine needles and dryer lint for tinder. small tinder stacked in the form of a tipi. *Note the black "Y" sticks- pushed into the ground to support the other upright sticks. This arrangement allows you to create a quick, hot fire that can be easily maintained by adding progressively larger kindling and then fuel. For best fire progression, add larger kindling, then dry softwood. To maintain the fire, add dry hardwood, a few pieces at a time- NOT all at once if you wish to preserve your fire for as long as possible.

This is a cross-section of a Cross-Hatch Fire. Notice how the kindling sticks are placed ALTERNATELY instead of right on top of each other. This allows for better air circulation thru each layer. Leave room for tinder underneath. This design produces a quick fire that is easy to maintain by simply laying wood in top (in progressively larger sizes) in the same alternating pattern with which you placed your kindling.   Air flow is shown by the red and yellow lines.

Outdoors Guy- The Hiking Trip and Viking Trip

One of the many best experiences of camping is getting out into the woods and exploring. I would always recommend following trails that have already been well traveled and marked out. The reason is simple. If you need to be found and returned, a well-established path is easy to find and follow, making the route for your friends or rescuers easier, and thus making you much easier to locate.

Have you considered leaving a trip plan with at least 2 reliable people who are nearby and can receive a text or cell phone call, or at least respond to your absence when you've gone past a reasonable time limit for your return? Do your friends know the area as well so they'll know where to go and look?

A trip begins with Preparation and Planning- not when you start walking. There should never be such an event as, "Let's get our stuff together and go hiking!" (O.K. Where? With whom? What supplies do we need to take? Does anyone have anaphylactic reactions to stings? Are their snakes? Wasps? When should we return in order to be safe and not get stuck? Are there any parts of the trail that are flooded/steep/rocky/muddy and narrow? How are we going to communicate if an emergency arises and we need assistance or if someone wanders off the trail and gets lost?)

This sounds like an awful lot of fuss and bother for just going walking, doesn't it? The truth is, the woods have to be respected. Accidents happen. Poor planning anticipates few if any problems, thus doesn't bring the proper equipment and take just plain common sense precautions. It just takes for granted. This can be a costly mistake. Naturally, if you know where you're going and familiar with the terrain, the trip will usually be fun and uneventful. But you can't count on every condition being perfect. The whole point of preparation is to empower you to be able to effectively handle emergency situations.

One memorable (sort of) occasion I recall was when I was out canoeing and heard a child very upset about yellow jackets. It soon became apparent that the hikers hadn't been aware that there was a yellow jacket nest close to the trail. The boy wasn't badly stung. All that it took was the presence of the yellow jackets, active during the daytime, and a few of them to land on him to cause him to become distressed. What child wouldn't be thrown by this unexpected fright? My point is this- what if you aren't prepared, and encountered this situation and someone in your party had an anaphylactic reaction to stings. Did you bring <u>at least</u> 1 Epi-Pen? <u>Preparation takes these critical factors into account</u>! (You should have enough Epi-Pens to keep someone's airways open until help arrives or you can get them out of the woods and get help.) *Alert the EMS Unit that you have an anaphylactic patient.

Granted, you can't always anticipate events like this. You may be the "first to know". <u>But be prepared</u>. You just never know so you put the odds as heavily in your favour AHEAD OF TIME as you can. Arm yourself with knowledge, develop a plan, carry equipment, don't worry, and handle incidents calmly. Seriously, give yourself as many cards to play with as you need. Carry a cell phone- charged- each person!

The Hiking Trip

Carry a cell phone! Wait, didn't I just say that? I want to make sure the point gets made. Now...what else do we bring with us? We'll divide the good stuff (our equipment) into 2 parts: what we can carry ON us and what we can carry in a knapsack or attached TO us. Here's my play on this…

You'll need a hat for shade and to shield your eyes, UV sunglasses (GOOD quality ones), a water skin, a hiking stick (extremely important), a belt knife or folding knife, compass and whistle, and a multi-tool. This equipment can either hang around your neck or be strapped to your belt, or placed in a pants pocket.

The walking stick and belt knife are CRITICAL pieces of equipment. The walking stick can help you avoid twisting or spraining your ankle, can serve as a staff for defense, it can even help get you out of quicksand! The belt knife is the key tool if you have nothing else if you have to survive outdoors for the night. It can help create a fire, make you feel safer since you have another weapon for defense, and help you construct a shelter by cutting branches. Most things you make from branches, etc. in the outdoors have to be shaped- hence a good, SHARP knife is absolutely essential.

I have (as mentioned elsewhere in this book) a combination whistle/compass/thermometer. One instrument can help me navigate, signal, and determine the temperature so as to dress, sit in the shade and rest accordingly.

Water is #1. Take as much safe drinking water as you can. Stop at regular intervals and take sips. My water skin holds 1L. And has a string that allows me to carry it around one shoulder.

My multi-tool was one of the best year end gifts from a student ever. This compact tool has a hammer, saw, knife and screwdriver blade and an opener. Imagine what this can do for you if you all of a sudden need tools.

Other Essentials: Carry 3 ways to make fire: matches, a lighter or 2, and a magnifying glass. Have some protein bars. Carry insect repellent and sun-screen. If you have a map, fold it and keep it in a side pocket to consult as needed. Know your landmarks and how to use the compass. Carry a flashlight and spare batteries. Carry a windbreaker and light rain suit. Carry a signal mirror or a CD for signaling and wear a bandana or bring a wash cloth to help cool off and refresh. MOST IMPORTANT: Bring prescription medications with you (a few day's supply), and a small first aid kit (fanny pack) just in case. I'd draw the line here if you're just going out for a day hike. Why bring a pile of equipment you don't need if you'll only be walking "there and back"? Concentrate on what you need based on what you plan to do and how far you plan to go. EVERYONE should have their OWN SET of basic equipment. This is first-line equipment.

For the adventurer, we can step it up a notch but we're coming to the point where you really have to decide how long and how far you'll be venturing. There are commercially available tents and sleeping bags that are light and compact. (Ask to see the "Biker's Tents" and sleeping bags at the local outfitters.) Or you might want to play it Old West style and bring a blanket roll. Add a Pilates mat then for making sleeping more comfortable. Are we loaded to the max yet? No? You're the rugged type, aren't you?

If this is, however, a planned over-night trip, we need to call in the reinforcements. NOW I'd carry my survival backpack. Hand and foot warmers, dried soup, first aid supplies (more of them, a metal cup and hexamine stove, hatchet, rope, a space blanket, orange garbage bags, spare fire starters, snare wire, a camp saw, mosquito netting, an emergency mylar shelter, soap, toothpaste, toothbrush, face cloth, water filtration equipment, a coat hanger...you get the idea).

Now you ARE well loaded down. But equipment has to match need and circumstance. The longer you are travelling, the more supplies you'll need to sustain yourself. My suggestion is- why not travel in pairs/small groups? That way someone else can take the backpack. The extra equipment is carried to SUSTAIN you for a longer period of time.

Having said all this, if you're going out overnight anyway, or you'll be travelling via water (you can see where this is going...) why not make this trip the...

Viking Trip!

This trip will brand you as a rugged adventurer. Think of the Norsemen exploring the wild new lands and braving the harsh conditions! The TRUE Adventurers! (BTW...don't take this too far- the Vikings could be a trifle on the obnoxious side...)

The advantages you now have are two-fold.

1. Let the canoe bear the weight of the equipment. You can now just take what you need without having to lug everything all the time.
2. You can now carry more food, water, fishing equipment and a better shelter.

*You also have an emergency shelter if you need it. My suggestion is to turn the canoe over at a 45° angle and prop it up at each end with a sturdy "Y" shaped stick. Over this you can drape a tarp and your old curtain sheers for mosquito netting. (*Mentioned earlier.)

AUTHOR'S NOTE: Anchor the canoe safely. Haul it in and turn it over if there's any risk of rain coming. As well, bring a tarp for covering all your gear. If you haul the canoe in and unload it, you still need to keep your gear dry. In a pinch, you can crawl under the canoe for shelter- about as "Viking" as it gets!

Did you remember the extra paddle, your lifejackets, rope? Good! You have the makings of a STELLAR Viking! Do you have a map? Do you know the water you're travelling on? Are there shallows where you'd need to portage? Are there rapids? Learn how to manage these ahead of time. Does EVERYONE have a cell phone- charged? (Great! Now you're one step ahead of your Viking brethren!)

To sum up:

-Always carry a complete set of first line equipment- as listed above.

-Gauge your need for equipment and thus how much you'll be carrying by the length of your trip and anticipated conditions.

-LEAVE A TRIP PLAN WITH AT LEAST 2 RESPONSIBLE PERSONS YOU CAN READILY COMMUNICATE WITH IF YOU NEED HELP.

-In the event of an accident- safety and first aid first. Then communicate where you are and request assistance. Be as specific as you can about your location- where you entered the woods and where you believe you are now. Carry and use communication and signaling gear.

This seems like so much to think about. It is, but it isn't. Once you establish safety and equipment procedures and become familiar with planning, it's routine. You have your equipment assembled and know what to do. That way, you have a much better opportunity to enjoy yourself and feel safer. Remember: The laws aren't meant to limit the people. They're there to protect the people. So is it with proper preparation for Hiking and Viking.

Peace Be the Journey ☺

Safe Be Your Landings- Often Be the Returning ☺

The next illustration really isn't me. I just never got beyond stick people in Art…

Outdoors Guy

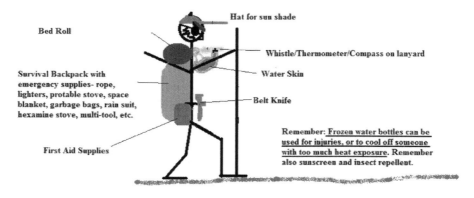

Me out Hiking: The Equation is: Necessary Equipment Divided by Weight. Too much or too heavy isn't good. So really plan ahead! Think about what you need and what equipment will "do the job" and yet still be portable- not to heavy or bulky. Here's where a "Biker's Tent" and Tube Tent really come into there own. *Space Saver Tip: Why not roll up your Pilates Mat and Blanket into ONE roll? **Remember Prescritpion Medications (Especially Epi-Pens)!!

Hat for sun shade

Bed Roll

Whistle/Thermometer/Compass on lanyard

Survival Backpack with emergency supplies- rope, lighters, protable stove, space blanket, garbage bags, rain suit, hexamine stove, multi-tool, etc.

Water Skin

Belt Knife

Remember: Frozen water bottles can be used for injuries, or to cool off someone with too much heat exposure. Remember also sunscreen and insect repellent.

First Aid Supplies

Outdoors Guy- Camp Cooking With The Family

This is just plain simple camp recipes along with some fatherly advice about doing things together. These recipes are tasty, simple, and easy. The keys are minimal preparation, simple ingredients, and...creativity. *Stay away from wild plants you're not sure of! Mind you...dandelions-though bitter- make a wicked salad with dressing. Use young leaves- cleaned.

Camp Chili

-1 can diced tomatoes

-1 lb. lean ground beef

-1 green pepper

-1 onion

-canned or fresh mushrooms

-garlic powder

-black pepper

-chili flakes &/or chili powder

-1 can red kidney beans

-1 can tomato soup

- dash of cumin (optional)

Brown meat in pot with onions & green pepper. Add all other ingredients and simmer for 1 hr. Season to taste when you add the canned ingredients. Great with cold beer.

Fish a La Grille

-2-4 healthy sized fish fillets (walleye, pike, crappie, perch, bass, rock bass)

-6 medium potatoes sliced in discs

-1 medium to large onion- sliced in wedges

-margarine or cooking oil

-large sheet of foil

-beer (optional- but GOOD!!!!!!!)

-Montreal Steak Spice (NOT negotiable)
-garlic powder

Line the foil with margarine or oil. Lay out the potatoes and fish fillets. Sprinkle fairly liberally with steak spice and garlic. Overlay with onions. Optional: pour in an ounce of beer before sealing the foil. Cook 10-15 minutes for each side depending on the size of the fillets. Turn once. Fish is done when it flakes easily with a fork.

Option: You can add baby carrots to this and do it up as a vegetable dish rather than a fish grille. Good for roasting corn too. Or, alternately, substitute chicken for fish.

Breaded Fish Fry

The trick to this one is to get the oil really hot by the time you add the fish. BE CAREFUL not to let the kids anywhere near the oil.

-fish fillets
-1 or 2 packets of no name chicken coating mix or bread crumbs in a large zip lock bag
-lemon pepper
-Montreal Steak Spice
-onion and garlic powder
-black pepper
-salt

The trick here is to add a little of this spice and a little of that spice and keep taste testing the mix dry until you like it. I like to be fairly liberal with the lemon pepper and especially with the steak spice- easy on the onion powder.

Take the freshly cleaned or fillets and place them in the bag full of bread crumbs. Shake until the fish is well coated. With fillets that have just been defrosted, dipping them in fresh milk helps restore the freshly caught taste. Lay the fillets gently into hot oil (about 1-2cm deep) and let the fillet BROWN (be patient). Turn once and let the other side BROWN. This will make the fillet crisp and gives the best texture and flavour. Serve with lemon or lime wedges, salad, your favourite rice dish or baked potatoes- beer or white wine to compliment.

This would certainly be one meal for a side dish of potatoes cooked with onions in foil or baked in the coals.

Spanish Rice

This is easy and pleasing.

-1 can diced tomatoes
-2 cups cooked rice
-chili powder
-black pepper
-can mushrooms (optional)
-1 can of sweet corn
-1 onion and green pepper diced and fried to soften.

Boil rice and partially fry the diced onion and pepper.

Add all ingredients to a pot- best if the tomatoes and corn are brought well heated first in the pot. Then you just stir in all the ingredients and season to taste.

Ol' Wild West Beans & Wieners

Sell it to the kids this way...I really don't know if there's anything really Ol' Wild West about it except visions come to mind of prospectors lugging around dried beans as a food source that would last them. Seriously, with this as your staple diet, no one within 5 miles would try and get near enough to jump your claim. But it is simple.

-1 pack of hot dogs- best roasted over smoky hickory fire.
-2 cans of beans slow simmered over a fire with chopped
-1 can of mixed or kidney beans.
-fried onions. (Optional)
-bacon to add some smoke flavor.
Taste test and add ingredients a bit at a time.

Cut the wieners up and add to the beans or serve separately on toasted buns. A good addition to this meal is sauerkraut- no, seriously.

Hobo Stew

The nice thing about Hobo Stew is that it can be a nomer for just about anything you have leftover. Think about having 1lb. of hamburger left, and a couple of cans of vegetable soup. An onion is still in the bottom of the cooler. Fry the hamburger and add salt, pepper, steak spice, garlic powder. Or make mini-meat-balls and fry them. Add the 2 cans of vegetable soup. Simple- but it's a meal. Try to steer the conversation away from adding things like dandelion leaves, etc.

Sloppy Joes or Tacos

These are easy and the kids (small AND large) love these- a perfect way to add variety to a lb. of hamburger. Prepare as for Hobo Stew and add pasta sauce. Maybe a dash of chili powder for the Tacos. No taco shells? Try tortillas!

Shish-kebabs

This is one of the best and easiest kebab recipes I've come across. IF you want to please the crowd, this comes as close as I'll ever get to a guarantee. (Notice I didn't say, "Money Back Guarantee"?) This starts at the dollar store- with bamboo skewers, so you KNOW it's a winner.

-onion wedges
-cherry tomatoes
-green pepper sections
-mushrooms
-beef strips and/or hot dog sections
-barbecue sauce (I love this with honey garlic, hickory smoke or even teriyaki sauce)

Simply skewer each ingredient onto your barbecue sticks and grill over a low fire. This is <u>YUMMY</u>! Make sure to baste each ingredient with sauce.

Poutines

Simple. Bake your potatoes in foil wrap- partially- enough to soften them up. Slice open the top lengthwise and add cheddar cheese and some bacon bits. Season to taste. Bake longer so the cheese melts. Best to pre-cook the bacon before adding.

Traditional Stand-By's

Grilled cheese sandwiches over a low fire. YUM! Even Macaroni and cheese with hamburger thrown in. Hot dogs are a MUST! (Mustard with relish and onions…YUM!)

Pancakes can be made more fun by bringing along some raisins or, just use some canned lunch meat- one slice in the middle of each pancake. Great with syrup.

Final Word…Remember that often times it's just as much about HOW YOU SELL what's for dinner with the kids. Cooked over an open fire is great to give a new twist to a routine, even boring meal. And let's face it, food DOES taste better cooked outdoors. There's always the enticement of S'mores and roasted marshmallows for dessert. We used to build an entire day around making First Nations "crafts" and then celebrating with nothing fancier than roasted hotdogs and canned fruit. And the kids loved it!

The fact that the outdoors is a change of scenery and pace from regular life at home is enough to add that touch of magic to even ho-hum stuff. Pretend you're back in the Pioneer Days. Let the older kids plan a meal. Most of all, share your TIME TOGETHER.

Plan in advance with 3 ideas in mind for camp cooking:
1. Simplicity
2. VARIETY
3. Enjoying this time as an adventure together (You can ALL prepare something for dinner and bring it all together at meal time.) Delegate meals. It doesn't have to be elaborate.

Share a few of your fave recipes with me in the next GNA??-it would be nice. Bon Appetite! In case of heartburn- supply own remedy. Keep the kids SAFE from any fire and anything heated over a fire. Always supervise!!. Make sure all meat is FRESH.

I am one of those people who believes that camp fire food is the BEST!!!!!

Make camp cooking, as well as all your other camping activities a SHARED experience.

Have Fun!! Life is too short to forget to do this most important thing.

Outdoors Guy

Let's move on to my favourite topic…I'll give you one guess…

Fishing

Outdoors Guy Introduction to Fishing

I figured I'd better mention fishing sooner rather than later. REMEMBER: you're preparing to tell your significant other about the tackle box you want for Christmas- the one with **three** trays... Now we HAVE to find some neat stuff to fill that lure box, don't we? (Con artist!) OK, let's start a crash course. Your significant other is going to give you dirty looks if you run the bill up at the bait store. This will sound like a contradiction but when choosing rods, reels and line, buy the best you can afford. You DON'T have to buy the latest high-tech and the most expensive top end stuff. Reputable brands like Shimano™, Daiwa™, Abu-Garcia™ have been around a while now for good reason- they make dependable products at a range of prices. Shakespeare's Ugly Stick™ is up to the task on the water. Good quality line pays off when you don't lose that fish (know how to tie a basic knot or 2 like a Trilene™ Knot or Uni Knot). Cheap equipment will disappoint you and let you down. So... we proceed with what we can do with a budget to still afford the best chances for success.

There are a number of lures which will serve to catch a variety of species. They've been on the market for a long time for one simple reason- they get results.

So, my basic line-up.

1. Rapala™ floating 9cm or 11cm. I favour natural colours-Perch. Natural Minnow, Yellow Perch, Brown Trout, Brook Trout. The best success I've had has been with a colour pattern called Chartreuse Rainbow. It's hard to find. This bait is universal. Use it as a go to bait. Try twitching the minnow and letting it float back to the surface as though crippled as well as a steady retrieve.

Countdown minnows in 7cm. work well. They sink 1ft. per second. Use them at varying depths.

2. Spinners. If there is one universal lure for freshwater fish-this gets my nod. Mepps™ 3, Blue Fox™ 3, Panther Martin™ 1/6 oz. or 1.4 oz. The Mepps™ Black Fury is excellent for clear water/low light. Mepps Comet™- white with red spots, red/yellow/black Aglia™ blade, chartreuse with black spots are my faves. 1/8 oz. Helin Roostertails™ are deadly for trout.

3. Spinnerbaits. 1/4 oz. size- white or chartreuse with a 3 in. twister tail as a trailer. Work these along the edge of large weedbeds. Pike and bass will take these if they're prowling.

4. Crankbaits. Remember! You can spend a fortune on lures! There are more varieties out there than you and I could afford in a lifetime- in 3 basic shapes. 1. Slender-Cordell's Walley Diver™ and Rapala's Tail Dancer™- Chub or Chartreuse Chub are excellent for walleyes. 2. Fat-bodied cranks such as Bomber™ 2A, 5A, 6A, Rapala's Fat Rap™, Cordell's Big O™ (I really like the perch design), and Storm Hot-N-Tot™ get my votes here. 3. Shad (flat-sided) such as Rapala's Shad Rap™.

5. Spoons. OK. I know what you're thinking. Red and white Dardevle™ for Pike (or yellow/red 5 of diamonds). You're right- they are deadly baits. However these aren't the ONLY spoons you can use effectively. A weedless spoon such as Johnson's Weedless Spoon™ with a plastic twister tail or plastic frog deserves serious consideration. These can be fished in, around, or over weed beds.

6. Lipless Crankbaits. Basically meant to mimic a shad. They have a tight vibration and fast wobble and weights inside to make noise. Cordell™, Bill Lewis™, and Rapala™ (I know- this name comes up a lot!) in 1/4 oz. are my best producers to date. Natural colours- try florescent colours in lower light or stained water.

7. Helin Flatfish™ X4 or X5- Frog, Perch, Sherbet Rainbow. Or Kwikfish™ K8 or K9. They have the most unbelievable wobbling action. Work them slowly- casting or trolling. They will catch a wide variety of species if presented properly. My Dad's favourite-my favourite.

All right- have we any money left before the budget is going to cause serious domestic problems? Almost done!

8. Top Waters. Calm surface in the evening or early morning. These are lethal worked along the edges of cover such as lily pads. Arbogast™ Hula Popper, Rebel™ Popper, Arbogast Jitterbug™, Heddon Torpedo™ and Zara™ Spook. A popper is a "still" bait. Cast it, let it sit, twitch the rod tip to pop it, let it rest, etc. A moving bait like a chugger (Jitterbug) or a prop bait (Torpedo) can be cast or trolled. For the sake of universality- stick to 1/4 oz. or 3/8 oz.

9. Soft Bodied lures- Mister Twister™, Berkeley™ Power Baits, Northland™Fishing Tackle's soft Grubs. I really like 3 in. twister tails on 1/8 to 1/4 oz. jig heads. Top colours- black, yellow, chartreuse, white or orange. I always rig these to a spinner blade for added flash and action. Effective for all species.*You can sometimes find these at dollar stores for bargain prices. Tube jigs and plastic worms 4" & 6" sizes also deserve serious consideration.

So we arrive at the counter with a floating minnow, spinner, spinnerbait, spoon, a crankbait or 2, a Flatfish, 2 or 3 different topwaters, a lipless crankbait, and a pack of twister tail grubs with jig heads. Not cheap, but will be enough of a variety to cover a lot of situations and species. HINT: Check bargain bins for brand names- seriously. Sometimes you'll be amazed.

FINAL NOTE: Don't scrimp on rods, reels, or line. Buy QUALITY line. Best for a variety of situations- 8lb. or 10 lb. limp line for smooth casting and strength. A 6'6" graphite rod matched with a reasonably priced spinning reel by Shimano™, Daiwa™, Abu Garcia™ or Shakespeare™and Trilene™ 8-10 lb. monofilament line is a good set up to start with.

For a few hundred dollars, you can make a start- rods, reel, line, baits, net, needle-nose pliers. Remember that lures were meant to hook us fisherman as well as fish- you could spend endless amounts of money. Starting with some basics will get you up and running and stay within the budget.

Now Go Fishin'!

Outdoors Guy- Tackling Topwaters

There are few thrills in fishing to match the moment when a bass or pike appears out of nowhere and smashes a top water lure. I love to hear the sound of a fish swiping at a lure I'm trolling 30 or 40 ft. behind my canoe. I particularly like it when a fish persists- missing the first few strikes yet daring enough to try it one more time.

Top water lure fishing is a fantastic tool in a fisher-individual's arsenal. I would hasten to say it isn't the only tool in their arsenal. Sometimes fish are down deeper at a more oxygen rich and cooler level (the thermocline level) and hanging on structures such as break lines and gravel bars. There are, however, times when hunger trumps comfort and aggressive bass/pike are prowling near a large area of cover such as an emergent or submerged weed bed.

Here are some of the top water all-stars and some ways to use them. Some are real classics. They've been around for decades and are still selling. Why? They continue to produce fish.

Arbogast Jitterbug™: This old timer can be cast or trolled. Use it, as you would any top water, near an area where cover seems to suggest ample hiding room for a predator fish. More later on cover. The Jitterbug splashes and gurgles like a mouse or frog trying to swim. You can retrieve it steadily or try a stop and go retrieve- reel it in, let it sit 5-10 seconds, then reel again. Experiment here. A Jitterbug is a cool lure to fish with because, you can HEAR it gurgling properly if it's action is right. You know you're trolling at the correct speed to present this lure properly. Thus, you don't have to turn your head every 2 seconds to check on it. Definitely turn around if you hear a splash and see your rod tip bend!

Arbogast Hula Popper™, Rebel Popper™, Cordell Popper™, Rapala SkitterPop™: This lure was designed to be cast and retrieved. You cast it alongside a surface weed bed or to the other side of a submerged weed bed. These lures have skirts of feathers or rubber that dangle in the water and irritate fish. Cast the popper out and let it land. Then begin a series of short jerks on the line to produce a "pop". Vary the rate and frequency of pops. Allow some time in between for a curious fish to take a look at the lure and muster up the courage to strike. My personal theory is that there are three basic responses to surface lures, other than, "No Thanks!" Fish will strike out of curiosity, anger, or hunger. No matter which one! Enticement is the name of the game.

Torpedo Lures- Heddon™, Cordell Crazy Shad™, Ozark Mountain™... These lures resemble torpedoes- hence their name. Since they give a steady action, they can be trolled or cast like the Jitterbug. I have caught crappies and rock bass with a smaller torpedo…and 4 lb. bass! There's a tip here. If you leave too much line out a behind your vessel, you run the risk of snagging weeds as you go around the point of a weed bed. You also may have too much slack in the line to set the hook properly owing to having so much line out. Estimate about 30-40 ft. If you are trolling, again, look for the edges of large weed beds or run the lure over a large rock pile. These are classic holding spots for bass, pike, and pan fish. Corners where there is access to deeper water can be very good. Hint: if the fish misses the first time, try again. Even go back and use a different surface lure. (Example: switch from a Jitterbug to a Hula Popper). No guarantees, but sometimes this does work. Try it.

Zara Spook™ & Rebel Frog-R™: These lures have no fins or blades to give it any action. You provide the action by simply twitching the rod tip lightly. This makes the lure dart from side to side. It gives a startlingly real imitation of a crippled minnow. Cast the lure out past the edge of a weed bed or alongside a weed bed and "walk-the-dog" (the name given to this technique). Vary your retrieve to make the action of the lure as erratic looking as possible.

Buzzbaits: These lures feature 2 or 3 large propeller blades and look very similar to a spinner bait. The difference is that a buzz bait will swim on the surface and cause a commotion. You have to reel or troll fast enough for the lure to rise and stay churning on the surface. These can even be worked thru weeds that aren't too dense.

Mann's Baby 1 Minus™ and Storm Sub-Wort™: I mention these along with surface lures because these baits are working either on the surface or just below the surface. They contain rattles which make them noisy and create a wake on the surface giving the illusion of fleeing prey. You've probably guessed where I'm going to recommend you use these but there's a difference here. These lures work where other lures may not- in very shallow water where you have a avoid fouling your lure on the weeds. If bass are hiding under lily pads they'll see this type of lure swim by. Larger predators are opportunistic feeders and strike if the presentation is performed to imitate natural prey. If you have little depth to work with and want to get sub-surface, give these a try.

The Unexpected Tool I would like to list may come as a bit of a surprise. Floating minnows. Yes, they swim at 2-6 ft. when retrieved or trolled, but have you ever considered them as surface lures. Minnows come into their own here as being so versatile. Cast the minnow out toward your target and twitch it like you would the Zara™. The lure will "dive" then struggle to the top like a wounded minnow. Leave it for a few seconds and repeat erratically. Crappies really like this opportunity to become predators in their own right. My preference for this type of presentation is a 7cm. To 11cm Rapala™, Cordell™, Bomber™, or Rebel™ minnow.

Weedless Spoons: Northland™ and Johnson's Silver Spoons™ are established names. They either have a skirt on the end or you just simply add a twister tail grub. These spoons feature a weed guard wire which allows you to fish them right over and thru the weeds. Look for pockets or cast over shallow submerged weedbeds.

Finally, a nod to the Heddon Lucky 13™. This lure does double-duty as a sub-surface swimmer with a wide wobble and as a popper. Use it in shallow water close to large areas of cover.

Well there it is. There are numerous colours and different makes of the same design. Why not choose 1 of each in either ¼ or 3/8 ounce sizes (I like the 3/8 oz. size Jitterbug because it makes more noise) and go try 'em out?

The biggest point of emphasis is that fish movements are daily and seasonal and that they have their preferred cover to hold in or around. Early morning and evening are productive times because of fish venturing further inshore to feed. Work LARGE areas of cover like lily pad beds (largemouth bass and pike), rock piles (smallmouth bass), fallen trees (crappies and/or bass). Work your lures over and alongside large submerged weed beds. (Cabbage, milfoil, coontail are known pike vicinities. Pike can also hide in the weeds waiting to ambush prey swimming by. The key is to look for large weeds in large clusters.) A point to make is that 1 or 2 isolated weeds does not a weed bed make. Look for LARGE areas of cover.

Topwater strikes take patience. You can get so excited by a strike that you yank the hook right out of the fish's mouth. If you feel or see a strike, wait a second, then set the hook. If the fish missed the strike, waiting and continuing your retrieve/troll may trigger them into striking again.

If it's mid-day, and top waters aren't producing, go down deeper. Early Fall (especially) can produce some amazing top water action because predator fish which normally hold in deeper water will venture into more shallow water to feed more often since the temperature and oxygen levels have now become more suitable. Later on, a bass's metabolism is going to slow down in colder water and they become more inactive. Smallmouth can tolerate colder water better than largemouth.

(BTW...Walleyes will, occasionally hit top water lures- but NOT VERY OFTEN! Take it as a bonus when a walleye hits one or your surface plugs). They are night time hunters, and prefer deeper, cooler water during the day. Another Also BTW...based on my results, pike seldom take top waters once it's dark. Bass will hit them after dark however- so don't give up trying if you can stand the bugs.)

It'll be fun getting to master the correct speed and action on your top waters. Just remember: Fishing is a combination of 2 basic factors: Location and Presentation.

Top 'O the Water T'Ye!!

Outdoors Guy

Outdoors Guy Rides Again- FISHING!!!!!!!!!!!!!!!!!!!!!!!

The tone at the outset of this article is going to have readers running for the doors. It all seems so complicated. Please bear with me because the whole point isn't to confuse you. The point is to organize and present some factors which have to be considered to catch fish consistently. It is focused on "fishing at the lake", or "fishing up at the cottage". It doesn't mention river fishing or fly fishing because I'm narrowing in on just, "going up to the lake", for now. The article's my longest one yet as it is.

I acknowledge, right at the beginning, the extensive knowledge and skill of my Editor Jim Shedden. Respect due by the Disciple to the Master. (However...the "Disciple" will be more than satisfied to get some credit...) If I say one thing, and Jim says something else...you decide.

Serious fisher-people, particularly competitive fisher-people, have to take these factors into account:

Water Temperatures and the Fish's Metabolism: Lake trout are active and comfortable in deep, cold water. 40-45 degrees

Fahrenheit. Largemouth Bass and Sunfish, on the other hand, can tolerate and actively feed in water around 70 degrees. Beginning with trout, which are more cold water fish, and going up the ladder thru Walleyes, then Pike, Smallmouths, to Panfish and Largemouths, each species has its own preference for temperature range. This in turn dictates, along with the fish's demand for oxygen, will dictate where fish will be located.

Daily and Seasonal movements: In Spring, spawning begins when water warms and fish become more active, For example, pike will gravitate to weedy, mucky back bays in relatively shallow water to begin spawning. The lake you fish on will have stratified into layers once the water has begun warming. Basically, the dark bottom of a relatively shallow lake will warm with the Sun's rays. When the deeper water warms up enough it rises- owing to the fact that warmer water is less dense than colder water. Hence the term: "Spring Turnover". The lake will stratify into 3 layers, the epilimnion (warmer, shallower, less oxygen rich water), the thermocline layer, and the hypolimnion. The hypolimnion is the lowest layer and may be very oxygen poor. Fish will be seeking the thermocline layer as being the most oxygen rich and having the most suitable temperature for their metabolisms. Depending on the size of the lake, the depth of the thermocline layer will vary. Imagine now, for a moment, that you're Superman with x-ray vision. From an aerial view you'd see fish scattered during summer. From a side view, you'll see them clustered. This isn't a contradiction. Fish will be holding on structures close to nearby cover where they can feed at night. Ideal "spots" are large areas of cover adjacent to nearby deeper water. In Summer, fish will typically move into shallower water in the early morning, drop back to the thermocline layer and to some deeper structure later during the daytime, and move in again in the evening to feed. In the Fall, fish will typically move into shallower water more frequently as the water temperature cools down and their instincts begin to tell them it's time to feed to prepare for Winter. Fall brings about the "Fall Turnover". Colder surface water sinks, and owing to the oxygen now circulating thru the lake, fish scatter more widely (at varying depths)since the thermocline layer doesn't exist anymore.

Structure and Cover: Structure refers to overall large contours of the lake bottom. Drop offs, reefs, gravel bars, saddles/humps, sinkholes, rock ledges, etc. It's hit or miss for a new fisherperson on a new lake without a contour map and depth finder. Even the pros get a day or 2 to practice on lakes before tournaments. Don't give up hope! Typically, certain species of fish will relate to preferred contours and types of cover. Drop off points and ledges with nearby access to shallower water and large weed beds or gravel bars, for instance, can hold large fish. During the day, they'll drop down and hold on a ledge (for example) in deeper water. Cover is the term used to describe what type of weeds, sunken trees, etc. fish use to protect themselves and use as bases for preying on food.

Lures: Catch a decent size fish or 2, and I guarantee that the first question you'll be asked is, "What're you using?" (As if this were the only factor- it isn't.) There are certain lures that have a reputation for certain species of fish. Then, I'll go out on a limb and say that there are certain makes of lures that are universal fish catchers for many species. However, certain lures are so associated with certain species that one is synonymous with the other. Mention the name pike, and images of red and white spoons come to mind- more on this later.

Equipment: Here's where you can spend a life savings or 2. And the gadgets change every year. There's always the newest item. I can't afford a $20 000 bass boat or $450 reels. The pros have to have this equipment because this is their livelihood. They also get endorsements from manufacturers if they win consistently. Don't despair. You should buy the best quality you can afford, but that doesn't mean top line.

If, by any chance, your head's starting to spin, I certainly can't blame you- Stratification, Seasonal Movements, Daily Movements, Structure, Cover, Equipment, Lure Selection, Water Clarity, Oxygen Content, Metabolism and Temperature.

My whole thrust in this article is to try and simplify a few factors, categorize them, and give you increased odds. Let's face it, vacation times limit us to a few weeks, we don't have tons to spend on every gadget, the display of lures, colour patterns, etc. is bewildering at a tackle store but we can't buy everything. (I can't!) So what if we looked at summarizing and condensing some information into a handy reference-sized space to help make your fishing a bit simpler and yet provide enough information to make you optimistic about next year's catch? Here's a way I suggest we approach the task. Let's aim for increasing the odds- just some basic guidelines. Just to shift the odds a bit more in our favour. I offer the following chart. It is meant to be a general guide only. It isn't a guarantee. Let's look at some preferred structures fish hold to, cover, movement patterns, lures with high rates of success, and some reasonable yet reliable equipment. I'm going by a self-imposed rule that says I have room for 25 basic kinds of lures in my tackle box to cover as wide a range as possible. Tall order? You CAN do it!! *I use brand names of lures with respect to their trademarks.

I'm focusing on Bass, Pike, Walleyes and Panfish. Musky fishing is specialized and not within the scope of this article. Similarly, Salmon and Trout <u>are</u> subjects for another article or 2 later. This focuses on, for the moment, "cottage country" fish. (*My own term.) IF you are situated in a section of cottage country near a secret trout stream, double bonus points to you!!! Just forgive me if I've narrowed the scope of my article- at least this time…What follows is a chart that aims to summarize fishing information.

Small Mouth Bass-Location(s) Look for them around rocks-home to crayfish which forms at least half of the smallmouth's diet. Large weed beds on the outer edges where they prey on smaller fish and frogs. Bonus Rock Bass may happen here too!

Try Using: Medium spinning tackle with 8 lb- 10 lb. line or lighter Baitcasting equipment. Use a crayfish imitation or bounce a 1/4oz. crankbait off of the rocks. Even bouncing the crankbait on a silty/rocky bottom will stir up mud and arouse the fish's attention. Size 3 spinners and 3 inch curl tail grubs work well. Tube jigs- resembling crayfish) are very effective.

Movements: Smallies move into shore in spring around rocks and gravel bars. They feed closer to shore during early morning and late evening- will suspend along rock ledges and drop offs during the day or under cover- and gradually move closer inshore in fall.

Large Mouth Bass- Location(s) May be found along or under large lily pad beds- even during the daylight. Will drop off into deeper structure during the day based on oxygen and temperature preferences. Bottom contours like humps and cover like large fallen trees, boathouses and docks.

Try Using: Medium – Medium Heavy spinning tackle. 8-10lb. clear or green line. *You may want to choose a line that has high abrasion resistance. Medium to medium Heavy Bait casting gear with 10-12lb. line. - Size 3 or 4 spinners. topwaters, 6 inch plastic worms (rigged Texas-style), 4 inch plastic grubs, weedless spoons, crankbaits from ¼ to ½ oz. with shallow, medium, and deep diving bills, imitation frogs- hard-bodied or soft-weedless, and floating minnows.

Movements: May be found along or under large lily pad beds- even during the daylight in summer. The key in summer is to locate areas where the contours change and the fish relate to deeper water where the bottom drops off. Fall may see action closer to shore but gradually diminishing as water gets cold.

Pike: Location(s): Weedy back bays in spring where water has begun to warm. Suspended in summer BUT may also be prowling around the outer edges of large weed beds anytime. Weeds to look for are broad-leafed species like cabbage, and milfoil. *Not just an isolated weed or 2- a large bed, especially where adjacent to deeper water.

Try Using: Medium to heavy Spinning or bait casting tackle with abrasion resistant line. The debate goes on since a lot of people used braided wire leaders as terminal tackle. I don't. I haven't lost a pike yet owing to shredded line from a pike's numerous teeth. The less indication you give of an artificial bait the better. MY OPINION ONLY! Spoons 2/5- ½ oz. White, chartreuse or black spinner baits, larger sized (3/8 to ½ ounce) topwaters, longer (4 ½ to 6 inch) minnows, twister tails, and size 3-5 spinners with buck tails. You can certainly go larger and heavier with Pike. 3/8 to ½ oz. minnow and crank baits. Pike aren't intimidated by the size of a bait. If they're feeding aggressively, they'll attack practically any bait if the presentation is right. Best not to go Musky size-again, my opinion- unless you KNOW you are fishing waters that hold monster pike and you KNOW where to locate them. These lures are GIGANTIC and you need water that holds monster fish along with the heavy tackle required to handle them. Again, this is a specialized type of fishing. ¼ oz. and 3/8 oz. lures will often get the job done even with 10lb. + pike.

Movements: Move into shallow back bays in the spring to spawn, then drop off into deeper water in summer and return to shallower water in the Fall. Pike are OPPORTUNISTIC hunters and may be found, even in the daytime, along the edges of large weed beds or even buried inside weed beds where they await prey. They rush out like a rugby player when they see food swim by. They are an aggressive, dominant species and often hunger can trump water temp.

Walleye: Location(s): Gravel bars, rock ledges and drop offs, underwater humps and saddles. These fish are mostly fish eaters and have excellent night vision. They will move closer into shore as darkness approaches. They prefer cooler water than Largemouth Bass and Pike. Temperature and oxygen content are important to walleyes.

Try Using: Medium Spinning gear. 8lb. test in clear or green is my choice here. A good quality reel with smooth dependable drag coupled with a good quality 6 1/2 to 7 ft. graphite rod gets the nod. Look for the combos on sale at your local bait and tackle store. You don't have to buy top end- but get the best you can afford. You won't be sorry! Size 3 spinners.Cordell Walleye Diver™, Reef Runners™, Rapala Tail Dancer™ or Shad Rap™/Cordell Shad™. 3 inch twister tail grubs!!! Again, for shallower water in low light conditions, the Rapala™/Rebel™/Cordell™ minnow is once again your universal go-to. Troll the minnow behind your boat, slowly and twitch it occasionally.

Movements: Walleyes look for deeper, cooler water at any time. Low light conditions may draw them into shallower water to feed.

Generally, stick to deeper, clearer water at any time and look for structure on the bottom that fish will relate to.

1 more tip. If you locate schools of baitfish in deeper water, you may locate walleyes feeding on them.

Panfish: Location(s): Near around under fallen trees, inside weed beds, under lily pads, around bulrushes. They're the prey for larger species so look for them where they would seek protection. They are trying to be inconspicuous. They will look for food in, or not far from, cover.

Try Using: Light spinning tackle or spin casting tackle. I don't use a bobber and worm, but this combo of a spin cast rod and reel, bobber, and worm has probably introduced more youngsters to fishing and being happy to bring home a few than all other combinations put together. Long, slender light or ultra-light rods really afford the most fun. Use light line. Even 4-6lb. Size 0 to Size 2 Spinners. Small spoons. Cricket, frog, crayfish imitations, small minnows, small tubes and curl tail jigs. It is a BLAST to catch smaller fish with mini and micro sized lures that mimic what a panfish naturally feeds on! You can find some very nice Panfish grub and twister tail kits at local tackle stores. South Bend™ makes some excellent soft-bodied bait kits. *See the related article on Ultra-Light Fishing for more detail.

Movements: I'll just say this- look for large areas of cover. These little critters are so often always willing to take a bait like a small minnow or worm or small spinner, spoon, or other ultra-light lure- but you have to locate them. If larger gamefish are the dominant species on a body of water, then panfish will be found in safer locations like weedbeds and among branches of fallen trees. *Note: Crappies will suspend during the summer and often in schools. These schools sometimes seem to be in the space of a bathtub at times. Locate 1 and you'll probably get more. The schools move around frequently so you really need a fish finder to locate them consistently.

This is long-winded, but there is so much that could be written- VOLUMES! I repeat- this is meant to give some general guidelines and tips. No insurance company would give a 100% guarantee. I've caught pike, walleye, lake trout… where they weren't "supposed to be." The largest brook trout in my record book was a 3lb. beautiful fish taken at the foot of a waterfall on a cheap imitation $1.99 lure!

So let's summarize. Fishing is a combination of 2 essential factors: **Location** and **Presentation**. What to use for what species where, when, how.

You may have noticed several lures that came up practically everywhere in my chart. I consider floating minnows, spinners, spoons, spinner baits, twister tails, and crank baits as universal lures. They cover the spectrum of a broad range of freshwater game fish. Vary the size of a floating minnow, and it can be used for any species. The same thing applies with a spinner.

*Please note that fly fishing is a time honoured, fun and specialized form of fishing- along with likely being the oldest form. I enjoy it and wanted to give it some special treatment in a later

article. I've written enough already. So, PLEASE don't be offended at not seeing fly fishing mentioned here. It's just 1 article.

I said earlier, and I mean to keep my word, that we could stock
the tackle box with 25 items or less and cover a wide range of
species and situations. Here's a tip. Baitfishes have, in general,
3 profiles. Fat and short (popular crank bait profile), broad and
thin (shad profile), and long and slender (minnows and lures like a
Cordell Wally Diver™). Since fish may suspend at different depths,
have at least 1 lure of each profile in your bag of tricks, and try a
few lures with difference size diving bills (the wider the diving bill-
the deeper the lure will dive). That way you can "cover the water".
Consider ¼ oz. to 3/8 oz. lures as a general rule of thumb. If you
know your water and what species you're going after- you can specialize your size and types of baits. If you're running on a REALLY
tight budget, at least include a Mepps™ 3 spinner, Rapala™ 9 or
11cm Floating minnow, a ¼ to 2/5 oz. spoon, 3 inch twister tail
rigged on a 3/8oz. jig head with spinner, 1 spinner bait, 3/8 oz.
chartreuse or white, and a crankbait or 2 to get down deeper.

I may suggest starting out by scouting out a lake. Look for
large areas of cover-locations where the structure changes, especially if there is a large area that drops into deeper water near
a large area of cover in shallower water. Fish relate to large structures. Try working the shallower edges around large areas of cover morning and evening, then go deeper over structural breaks
in the daytime. Obtain a contour map if you can.

As a final word (some of you are saying…F-I-N-A-L-L-Y!), you
can do it all right and lose the fruits of your labour with 3 simple
indiscretions. Line must be new. Line with a powdery surface has

decayed (likely due to UV exposure) and must be discarded. Use QUALITY line!!!! Berkley's Big Game is around $12 a spool and you get a LOT of line for the price. Use a proven knot to secure your line to a snap swivel. If you feel nicks or frays as you run your fingers over the terminal end of your line- cut off and re-tie! I have used the Trilene™ knot for 25 years. Simply loop the lead end thru the eye of a snap swivel or hook eye TWICE, wrap the line 5 or 6 times around, and bring the loose end (tag end) back thru the double loop. Moisten the knot with saliva and draw tight. Think: "2-6-1"- 2 loops, 6 winds, 1 draw thru. Finally, sharp- . en every hook with a sharpener or whetstone. Sandstone is best in a pinch. Your hook will be sharp enough when it "sticks" or can run a groove into your finger nails. These small things matter! You need to give yourself every advantage you can get!

I'd love to send this out with written guarantees. Can't do it! I begin writing this article even wondering if it was possible to summarize some key ideas into a small enough space to be read in 1 sitting and yet still cover a general spectrum. I don't fish for a living- I fish for fun. If even 1 or 2 things here give you an idea, if it works out for you a few times and you bring one home to brag on, if you learned a few things, I'm happy with that! Remember, we all have our own ideas and theories. Why not share some of yours with me? Tight Lines and Get Out There and Enjoy!!!

*I'll list all my "Top 25" in a moment, but let's have a bit of fun. Why don't you write down your Top 25 and then we'll compare notes…deal?

Only 1 box to fill and the Finalists are…May I have the envelope please?

Rapala Floating Minnow™ 9 or 11cm, Rapala Countdown Minnow™ 7cm, Cordell Wally Diver™, Daredevle™ Spoon 2/5 oz, Mepps™ 3 spinner, Spinnerbait with plastic trailer, Northland Slurpee™ or Mr. Twister™ 3" twister tail grub on 3/8oz jig-head with spinner, Storm Thin Fin Shad™, Lindy Shadling™ or Cordell Shad™, Rapala Fat Rap™ or Bomber 2A™ Crankbait, Jitterbug™ 3/8 oz., Hula Popper™ 3/8 oz., Zara Spook Puppy™, Luhr-Jensen Bass Oreno™ or Heddon Lucky 13™, Earie Dearie™ or Storm™ weight forward spinner 3/8 oz with plastic twister tail trailer, Headon Torpedo™ ¼ or 3/8 oz., Rebel™ Crayfish, Frog, and CrickHopper, X5 Flatfish™ or K9 (or K10) Kwikfish™, Lindy Shadling™ (this is one of those lures in a class by itself in my opinion- the colour patterns are amazing), Smithwick Deep Diving Minnow™, Lipless Vibrating Crankbait (Rapala™, Strike King™, X-Caliber™, Bill Lewis™, Cordell™...so many brands to choose from...), Johnson Weedless Spoon™ with trailer, and Storm Sub-Wart™ or Mann's Baby 1-Minus™ for just under the surface along weedbed edges.

There! I promised 25. Trying to cover different depths, species, and situations such as type of cover, and what each species likes to dine on. I've shared a lot of information with one exception...

One of Canada's most beloved outdoor writers, Gregory Clark, once said, "A sportsman is one who not only will not show his own father where the best fishing holes are but will deliberately direct him to the wrong ones." -from a speech to the Empire Club of Canada in 1950. The second most frequent question I'm asked is, "Where'd you get that fish?" To which my reply is always, "In the lake." (Which <u>IS</u> true, after all.) Hey, I'm an outdoors guy. Some things are sacred.

Your Pal as Always,

Outdoors Guy

Fly Fishing and Baitcasting- The Noble Arts

There are no two more disparate types of freshwater fishing, yet I esteem them both. You really can "catch on" to both of these- and they'll catch on to you too!

Fly Fishing

This is, according to my knowledge, the most time honoured form of fishing, save for spears and traps. This article is to introduce fly fishing. Volumes are written about this art. I can cover some beginning instruction in the space available. Here we go. Fly rods and fly lines are weighted according to size and weight. Very light, shorter rods use lighter fly lines.2,3. Heavier rods use 8 or 9 weight line and are the right size to handle large trout, steelhead, salmon, and pike. For all around fishing, a 5 or 6 weight rod and line are good.

My reel is a Scientific Angler's™ single action fly reel. Single action in the sense that there are no gears that multiply the amount of line you reel in when you turn the handle, like there would be on spinning reels. My reel also doesn't have a drag.

You can start from here and move "up" by adding additional features you want when you are buying a reel. "Automatic" reels are spring loaded and reels now have drag systems. When I was taught to fly-fish, I was shown how to "palm" the reel, or to provide drag by pressing my palm against the spool.

A reel will start with backing. This is braided Dacron line (50 to 100 yards) and serves to give you additional line length should you be fighting a fish making a long run. Now we come to the main line. In fly fishing the weight needed for casting is in the LINE, not in the lure- as with spinning and bait casting, Lines are designed to match the size of your rod. Look on the rod to check what type of line to match with it. My rod was designed for "5 weight" line. Line can be expensive, so stick to an entry quality line of you're just starting. Look on the box and you'll see, typically, a label such as "WF-5" or "L-5". These mean: "Weight Forward" (the design), and "5" (the size/diameter of the line). "L" means "Level" (no taper at the end of the line). To go a step further- other initials tell you whether the line will float or sink. "WF_5-F" means, "Weight Forward- 5 weight line- Floating." The line used for dry-fly fishing. Try this…"WF-5-S"…"Weight Forward-5-Sinking"? (Good!)

The lines may also say fast sinking, extra fast sinking, or, "ST" (Shooting Taper)- which has a heavier forward end for making distance casts. My suggestion is to start with Floating line for shallow fishing since you have to have an accurate knowledge of the bottom of a body of water if you're going to use sinking line. If the bottom is weedy, the fly can collect weeds easily. Weight Forward Floating line allows you to cast farther than Level line and is suitable for starting out fly fishing and/or trying out new waters.

*Knots for joining backing to fly line are included below.

We are getting down to the business end of the line now. Still 2 pieces left to complete the whole set-up. From the tip of the fly line to the actual fly there is leader material. Sold in separate smaller spools. I have used just regular monofilament as well. I usually use 3 ft. of 6lb. leader. For smaller trout/panfish, 4lb. I use an attachment called a "No-Knot Eyelet" You can loop and tie the end of your fly line and then tie leader material around it, but I just think an eyelet is simple and uses less off the end of my fly line. Simply push the eyelet into the end of your fly line. It has small barbs that hold it.

FINALLY, we can tie on our fly. There is a school which says, "Match the Hatch." Meaning use dry flies, nymphs (immature larvae of insects) which match the creatures fish are feeding on. There is a school of thought called, "dredging" which makes use of nymphs and streamers (minnow imitation flies) to get down to the fish ("where the big ones are hiding"). And here we can start complicating matters again! And you're thinking..."NO!!! Can't this just be simple??" Agreed... I suggest starting out with a small assortment of flies with a few from the following categories:

Dry Flies*: Royal Coachmen, Wulffs, Duns, Cahills, Irresistibles...

Wet Flies: Parmachine Belle, Montreal, Gold-Ribbed Hare's Ear, Professor...

Nymphs: Hare's Ear, Zug Bug, Stone Fly...

Terrestrials: A grasshopper imitation, ants,

Streamers: Mickey Finn, Muddler Minnow, Grey Ghost, Woolly Bugger, Woolly Worm.

Crustaceans: These have small "eyes" and make deadly imitations of crayfish to fool Smallmouths.

PLUS: My trout trick…Go to the hobby store and buy a pack of pom poms. Little orange/pink balls made from acrylic. They have a fuzzy, glowing appearance that mimics a fish egg beautifully. Thread onto a size 8 or 10 hook and add a scent. They sink slowly to entice trout to bite.

*Note: Dry Flies have to have a floatant applied to stay on the surface. Available in small bottles- use just a drop.

The knot I recommend for tying flies to the leader is the Trilene™ Knot (Explained in the Introductory Fishing article.)

Almost there! To place a fly where you want it you have to learn to false cast. This means laying out more line progressively until you reach the desired length of line that covers the distance you want your fly to travel. It's easier than it looks. Old Timers used to teach novices to tuck a $5 bill under their armpits while casting in a fast-moving stream to emphasize not using your arm- just have to relax and use your wrist. Strip out a few feet of line and cast BEHIND you until it straightens out. Meanwhile, during the back-cast, you're pulling more line off the reel. Cast forward and keep holding out more line so that each false cast is longer. You're progressively letting out more line until you have enough to hit the target. *With each false cast the line must fully extend and straighten out! Your last cast is the real one. You've got enough fly line extended on your false casts that now you can lay the line forward onto the water. Let the fly settle, and work it in a series of short jerks while you gather the fly line in in loops around your other hand. You'll get used to it! Reel the line in and start false-casting again.

For areas with dense branches, you can "roll-cast". Distance is extended by lying out some line on the water, pulling more line off the reel, then by snapping your rod tip down, the line "rolls" in a wave on the surface of the water- the momentum carrying out more line. (Tricky at first.)

Folks with a passion for this really have a <u>PASSION FOR THIS</u>! Flies and fly typing have an incredible appeal. A well tied fly in itself is a masterpiece. There are so many BEAUTIFUL patterns to admire and…buy… Devotees collect flies for a hobby, or create their own. You have the rest of your life…why not collect a few at a time? Ask your sales rep. at the tackle store. Buy a dozen or so of classic patterns to work with. Ask for help getting set up with a starter selection. If you can gives the sales person info about what you're fishing for and what the water is like (e.g. shallow pond), it'll help narrow down the selection process. Remember to match the size of the rod with the reel and get advice on lines, backing, leader material, eyelets. Ask about knots too.

This could start you out on a passion that'll last a lifetime. It … is… SO…MUCH… FUN!!!!!!!!!!!! As mentioned in my Introduction, my wife bought me a complete starter set for trout fishing and I had a BLAST! I'll bet you will as well.

*Next: The Noble Art of Baitcasting…Stay Tuned…

Baitcasting- The Noble Art

Baitcasting got into my system this year- Big Time. I'd been using spinning gear for so long but I was intrigued about learning this new skill. The lure of fishing is basically that it always lures you. My wonderful family bought me gift certificates from my favourite tackle store as Christmas presents and the owner ordered me a matching Pflueger™ Baitcasting combo. Here's where quality not only in sales, but in service, really marks a retailer. My friend Steve took the time to give me a detailed lesson on how to use bait casting equipment. THAT'S service! His lesson was so good that I had essentially mastered casting with it in 15 minutes.

So, off to my favourite lake to try it out- I was **really excited**.

A bait casting reel seems to go up in gadgetry (and price) almost without limit from an entry level. From what I've read, there reels upwards of $450 with 32 computer settings designed to precisely calibrate reel functions. This is, I frankly admit, a little on the steep side for me- great for the pros and amazing technology. I got a good deal on a quality entry level outfit and I've been very happy with its performance. So I'm satisfied.

Let's start with some basic understanding of the controls on a bait caster. The spool tension knob allows you to control…spool tension. The problem with bait casting reels from time immemorial was how to avoid over-run on the reel, which resulted in the mess known as "bird-nesting"- a nasty hopeless tangle of line produced by the reel peeling off line faster than the lure was taking it out. Old time reels simply had a "clicker" on them and you tried to control the cast using your thumb. Modern advancements have added terrific features to bait casting reels that virtually eliminate this problem. The spool tension is one such feature. I was taught to tighten the spool tension knob completely. The next feature which works to control the spool is the…

Magnetic brake: This "fine tunes" the amount of control over the spool revolving. Again, it was stressed that I start at a higher setting. The settings run from 1-10 with 10 being the maximum amount of braking on the spool. These reels were designed for at least 3/8 ounce lures. I use it for 3/8 oz. and ¼ oz. lures. Lighter lures won't carry line out far enough- better to use spinning tackle.

The most important part of my lesson was how to gauge when the tension has reached the optimum point where you get maximum casting distance and control over the spool to prevent over-run. The lure on your line should JUST drop SLOWLY (about 2-3 ft. per second) when you release the line. Then the tension is right. If the lure doesn't drop, ease off on the brake setting until it just begins to drop. There is fine tuning always going on to get the tension right.

Now we've got the tension adjusted. It's time to use the thumb bar. Press it all the way down and hold it, like you hold your line when using a spinning reel. Bring the rod behind your head for your back cast and feel the rod tip "loading". This is a smooth, fluid motion, NOT a swing back and jerk. It should be second nature if you've fished with spinning gear. Bring the rod tip forward and release the line just before you get to 12 o'clock. I find that this slight adjustment in my cast gives me more casting distance. It's a fine line between 12:02 and 12:00. You should have released the line by 12:00 or the lure will travel down.

At this point your thumb becomes your best friend. Watch the lure and line. At the moment when the lure is JUST ABOUT TO HIT THE WATER, jam your thumb on the spool. If you're too late the line will continue peeling off and you will have your bird's nest. With a little practice, this becomes second nature. Engage the handle and the thumb bar will snap back into place- meaning you now have tension on your line and can reel. bait casting reels typically have high speed retrieves- given that they have high gear ratios. (Example: 6 revolutions of the spool taking in line for every 1 turn of the handle.) This means you have to watch your retrieval speed and match it to the action of a lures. A wide wobbling lure will likely mean you should slow your retrieve down. A lure with tight action- fast wobble- can be retrieved faster. You also have to remember to present lures at different speeds depending on the mood of the fish. If they are generally aggressive, you can use a faster presentation.

The rod will be a medium heavy to heavy action, stiff rod. Flexible, but the action is stiff and fast to enable you to set a hook with authority- the exact opposite of a noodle rod. It is in this situation that bait casting outfits shine. You can refine your casting to the point where you could almost hit a dinner plate at 40 yards. You also have considerable winching power in the reel.

The last feature we'll discuss is the star drag. This is positioned under the handle and adjusts to allow a fish to run without breaking your line, yet provides resistance to tire the fish out. You may have adjust "on the go" depending on the size of the fish and what you have to steer them away from (like weeds or branches).

Check the manufacturer's specifications on the rod and the reel for the recommended range for lb. test line. Rod and reel combo's are designed to be balanced. I use 10lb. limp line on my reel. This is probably as light as it goes for these reels. Gauge the need for heavier line by the size of fish you're pursuing and how heavy the cover is on your lake. You may need a line with higher abrasion resistance, in which case, look for "tough" lines rather than "limp/casting".

As a bonus, this year, a neighbour sold me an Abu Garcia Black Max™ reel with a graphite rod last summer... OK. The results- a 3 ft. pike with the Abu Garcia equipment. 2 weeks later, a 40 inch pike with my Pflueger outfit. Using top waters- a ½ oz, brown/orange Arbogast Jitterbug™ and an Ozark Mountain Woodchopper™ (prop bait). So I am SOLD forever on bait casting.

FINAL NOTE: People passionately love their specialized form of fishing. It's a matter of respect that we can appreciate someone who does it differently than we do. Methods differ like noodle rods and ice fishing rods- but FUN doesn't! It's like Canada- we celebrate each other's respective differences as all contributing to a great whole. So is it with Fly Fishing, Baitcasting, Spin

Casting, Spinning Gear, etc. We're just out having fun, maybe even discovering a new form of fishing that ADDS to our fun. Now THAT is Fishing.

Gotta Love 'Em All...

Outdoors Guy

Outdoors Guy- Hook, Line, and Sinker

This article is meant to hook the fish, "Hook, Line, and Sinker". When you think about it, the line, sinker and hook are where the business happens. We'll be discussing "rigs"- configurations of hooks, lines and sinkers. Certain rigs devised for certain specific situations.

Let's begin with the...**Texas Rig**. Developed in the U.S. for fishing Largemouth Bass in heavy cover, this arrangement is both simple, and very effective. Place a "bullet sinker" onto your main line and then tie on a "worm hook". The bullet's "nose" should be pointed up the main line/away from the worm. This sinker does 2 things: 1. It allows the bait to sink into pockets and allows you better control over the worm while you're working it. 2. The bullet head shape helps increase the weedless nature of this rig. Worm hooks with bent shafts are specially designed for fishing with plastic worms. I may suggest a size 1/0 or 2/0 hook as your all around go-to's. Then thread the plastic worm onto the hook with the point ANGLED into the head of the worm at 45° and pull the worm thru. Now the next step is important. Bring the head of the worm all the way to the eye of the hook. Rotate the hook a half a turn and embed the point into the body of the worm. Run the point of the hook thru the worm several times so you have enough of a hole for the hook to slide thru easily when a fish takes the bait. Make sure, after having created the hole thru the worm, to embed the hook so that the point is just inside the body of the worm. With the hook not exposed, this bait becomes almost completely weedless. The worm can now be cast into weeds such as lily pads and worked thru them by twitching the rod tip up and down. When you come to a promising looking hole in the weeds, twitch the worm and then let it fall for a few seconds- repeat. At one time it was emphasized that you had to set the hook so hard into the fish that you'd "cross its eyes". People started getting bills from fishes' optometrists! The thought is, however, to wait momentarily and certainly to set the hook firmly. If all goes well, the hook (which has to be "sticky-sharp" will easily slide thru the body of the worm and set. Plastic worms come in delightful flavours such as sow, garlic, licorice and salt.

I use 4" to 6" SOFT plastic worms for this type of fishing. The softer, the more easy to set the hook. Generally you can think 4" worms with a twister tail for Smallmouth Bass, and their longer 6" cousins for Largemouth Bass. Culprit™ Makes worms with an undulating ribbon tail. The action on this bait is awesome! The plastic is super-soft and the tail is, well, just simply enticing! It's just my opinion, but the larger 8" - 12" worms used in the Southern U.S. are a bit over-sized in Ontario waters where the Northern strains of bass don't reach the gigantic dimensions of their Southern cousins. The growing season isn't all year round, so they don't grow all year, as do Southern strain Bass. Mind you, that doesn't mean we don't hook trophies. We just tend to think of 5-6 lb. Bass as trophies. Yes, (sigh) they DO grow bigger in Texas! (And California, Georgia, Tennessee, Kentucky, and Florida...)

We now come to...**Drop Shotting**. This brings to mind a lazy afternoon when another camper came along with the same "ton of stuff" as me. The poor victim of the ensuing conversation (about every fishing technique known to human kind) was one of my best friends who just happened to have her campsite stuck between us "experts" (tongue in cheek). She put up with us yakking <u>for 2 solid hours</u>. (I wasn't about to outdone in "knowing my stuff". We have our pride you know...) I have some amazing (and PATIENT) friends.

We got on to the method of Drop Shotting. This involves a plastic worm of 4" which we wish to place near the bottom. To try and explain it simply- this is a "3-way" rig. Start with your main line and imagine a bell sinker tied on at the end, to get the bait to the bottom. Now, about a foot up from the bottom comes a 3-way swivel. There are 3 eyelets. Tie the main line to the top eyelet. Run a trailer line from the bottom eyelet to the desired length at which you want your bait to be trailing over the bottom. Tie a bell sinker onto the trailing line. This will get you bait down and also let you know when the rig hits bottom. The remaining eyelet runs out to the side. To this you attach your bait line with a hook and plastic worm (or grub). This can be slowly trolled behind the boat and gently worked up and down. Of course, you can vary the depth of your bait to find out where fish may be holding.

There are variations to this idea. Bottom Bouncer sinkers allow you to detect bottom while keeping your presentation/bait suspended and help protect against tangles with weeds. They provide a second eye thru your fingertips about the bottom.

Slip Sinker Rigs allow you to get bait down to a desired level-similar to my egg-sac rig in the Salmon and Trout article. Run a bullet sinker thru your main line and attach a swivel. Onto the swivel attach just a plain leader line with hook and bait OR... increase the action and attraction by using s spinner rig. These rigs feature spinners in silver, gold and highly colourful painted patterns which add attraction and vibrations to alert fish to your bait. This is a classic Walleye rig- used with live night crawlers and often featuring a "stinger-hook" further back to get those light biters. Since I stated before that I don't use live bait (it's just me...) I use 4" soft plastic worms with curl tails and/or 3" twister tail grubs.

As a final thought: Jig heads are a hook and sinker all in one. My favourite Walleye bait- but I've caught beautiful Largemouth and Smallmouth Bass with them, as well as 10 lb. Pike and a respectable host of Crappies. A ¼ or 3/8 oz. jighead tipped with a 3" twister tail in white, black, orange, yellow, purple or chartreuse is really a universal bait. There are a lot of stores (even dollar stores) have packages and packages of brand name twister tails for a dollar or two. I ALWAYS use a spinner on my jigs to add action and flash.

There ARE some jigs like Blue Fox Foxee™ (great for a cray-fish imitation for Smallmouth) and Lindy Fuzz-E-Grub™ (a Walleye staple) which were designed to be fished vertically. The Fuzz-E-Grub can be tipped with a minnow or fished without

OK. Get out there on the water and Go Get 'Em!

Outdoors Guy

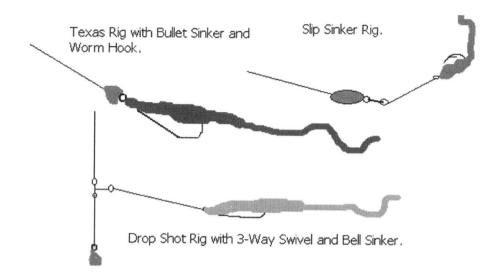

Texas Rig with Bullet Sinker and Worm Hook.

Slip Sinker Rig.

Drop Shot Rig with 3-Way Swivel and Bell Sinker.

For the Fishing Time of Your Life- Go Micro

It happened as I was just becoming a young teen- the mini craze of the 1960's. Everything was mini and micro. Ahhhhh, the good old days... It doesn't all have to disappear. Fishing seems to store many aspects of life while fashion and fad blow thru like a strong wind and disappear. So it is with micro lures.

This type of fishing has a lot to be said in its favour.
1. You can carry a tackle box full of lures in your pocket.
2. It's a riot.

3. Often you can bring home a stringer full.
4. Micro sized lures have a widespread appeal to numerous species of game fish. It may be THE place where trout meet panfish. Trout like little critters.
5. Ultra-lite equipment provides some of the ultimate excitement. You have to play a fish more carefully. The rod is super flexible and bends like crazy- action to appeal to youngster and the "other end of the chronological spectrum" as well.
6. You don't have to spend a fortune.
7. Often, limits on these fish can be very generous because they can take over a lake if they reproduce too proficiently. (Conversely, larger fish can begin to disappear if you take their food base away so try to keep a balance. Are you REALLY going to cook up 100 fish?)
8. It can fill the bill on a day when larger fish are nowhere to be found.
9. Great eating.
10. Not so challenging as larger fish-as long as you can locate them.
11. May more often be found in shallower water near shore since they don't want to venture too far from protection.
12. You set yourself up as a specialist- an aficionado of ultra-lite. (Instead of…"Oh, so-and-so had to settle for sunfish and rock bass!" No Sir/Ma'am!! You SPECIALIZE in this form of angling-so there!!! Nyah!!)
13. In consideration of #12, it is nice not to come home skunked.

14. 2 or 3 decent sized panfish make a very respectable meal.
15. Sometimes you can get a large surprise. Larger fish will hit smaller lures so be prepared just in case. (New line, Drag properly adjusted...)
16. Smaller fish of necessity have exist in greater numbers than larger predator fish to maintain their numbers and support the energy demands of higher order game fish.
17. You don't need a $20 000 bass boat.
18. If you can get into a school, the action is steady.
19. Panfish are a much better target if you're introducing a youngster to fishing. Very often, they don't care about waiting all day for the big one- they are thrilled just to catch one. The wide grin is worth it!
20. It is easy to adapt fly fishing for trout to fly fishing for pan-fish. They're still light lures.

You can hike into some great ultra-lite fishing spots and not have to carry piles of gear. An ultralight rod and reel set (good quality), trout net, and a hip box full of spinners and critter imitations.

My lure box has an imitation: crayfish, floating minnow, lady-bug, cricket/grasshopper, frog, shad, bumble bee, sinking min-now, spinner bait, 2 spinners and 2 spoons. Mepps™ 1, Worden's Rooster Tail™ 1/8 oz. and Panther Martin™ 1/8 oz. spinners really shine here. I have a trout classic called a "Super-Duper"™ and a few Blue Fox Spinning Minnows™. The idea is simple. Have imi-tations of what the fish are feeding on. They eat frogs, crayfish, minnows, insects, and grubs. So just bring some imitations and a few universal lures (like spinners) and you've got a respectable variety to offer.

It may be said that panfish are generous little munchkins. They are usually curious and willing to biters. They are usually not the top order predators on a lake so you have to look for them in spots they are using to hide in. Weed beds close to shore, downed trees with plenty of branches and around rocks. These fish will relate to cover. They are feeding on smaller prey than larger fish while trying to avoid becoming prey. So, again, ask yourself, "What are the smaller food sources for smaller fish?"

For a rod and reel you can use anything from a 4 ½ ft to 6 ft. Light or Ultralight spinning outfit. Since you don't expect a sunfish to spool off all your line on a defiant run, use 4lb. to 6lb. premium quality line. I stick by Trilene XL™, Cabelas' ProLine™, and Bass Pro's Excel™. limp- which makes for great casting distance, strong, abrasion resistant, with excellent knot strength. My suggestion for terminal tackle is a size 10 black snap swivel with a "U" shape and a bend at the point you fasten it to prevent the snap from coming apart. Use the smallest snap swivel you can- black because it is less visible to fish than brass.

A Few Tips:

-Smaller ponds may not contain larger fish but maintain a healthy population of sunfish.

-Rock Bass will characteristically making a distinct "slurping" sound as they try to suck in a surface lure. They'll likely give it a few tries then stop so as not to wander far from cover. If you miss one, go back and try again! They like to bite.

-Crappies will typically move around a wide area of a lake and the trick is to locate the school. A side-finder sonar is a huge help here. If you hook one crappie it's likely that you've gotten into the school and will hook more if you cast or troll thru the same area. Sometimes I could have sworn that the fish were stacked up in an area no larger than a bathtub at a resort hotel.

-Springtime is good for twitching a small floating minnow in shallow water beside weeds crappies are using for cover. Twitch, let the lure float back to the top, wait, twitch again.

-If the twitch/crippled minnow trick is working in one area in the spring, try another area with similar features.

-Large submerged brush piles and trees with a generous amount of branches are good places to use small tube jigs and grubs. Anchor in close by and dangle the jig as close to their noses as you can.

-Sunfish can make you believe you have a whale on the end of the line! They give a good account of themselves. Enjoy the sport. I don't use live bait but if you are going to use live bait for sunfish, a long-shanked hook such as an Aberdeen hook is a must since these fish will swallow the bait right down. You need a long hook shank to make it easier for needle nose pliers to remove the hook. If it comes down to a choice between life and limb and you're releasing the fish, instead of forcing the hook out, and doing real damage, cut the line. From what I've been told, the acids in the fish's stomach will dissolve the hook in a few weeks.

-Last Tip: Crappies have thin mouths so setting the hook hard enough to cross their eyes will usually result in just pulling the hook loose and tearing the fishes mouth. E-A-S-Y!

Flies like a Woolly Worm and Woolly Bugger are excellent for panfish. As well, any fly that mimics a crustacean, nymph, small minnow or insect will work. Again: match what they're feeding on.

So there we have it- the Art of Ultralight. (We've got plenty of Arts now.)This is enjoyable fishing. On a good day you get to come home with your head held high, boasting a respectable stringer, a wide grin, a few photos, feigned modesty, some "Ooooooooo's and Ahhhhhhhh's", and a fine dinner afterwards. Who can beat that?!

Outdoors Guy

Outdoors Guy- Stream and Pond Trout- The Jewels of Fishing

Stream and Pond Trout are among the most delicate jewels of fishing. Brook Trout rate in my mind as the prettiest fish (and the most delicate) fish anywhere. This article is dedicated to the sport fish of dreams- the 1 lb. to 4 lb. stream and pond trout- Rainbows, Brook Trout, and Brown Trout.

Since I've already written my Fly-Fishing article, forgive me if it seems like I'm overlooking it. The heart and soul of many trout fisher-persons lives for opening day on the trout stream. This article is intended to supplement the Fly Fishing article with light spinning gear and lures used for these beautiful creatures.

Stream and pond trout are very fly, minnow and nymph oriented. They eat smaller prey than their full grown, larger cousins who've been out in large, open water bodies. A steelhead (open water rainbow) is a good example. It reaches a healthy size when full grown and seeks LARGE prey to satisfy its energy demands. A diet of nymphs and small flies would equal starvation for a fish this size.

So going back to the Fly-Fishing article, flies are designed to mimic what a trout is feeding on- flies, crustaceans, nymphs, small minnows. So it is with my jewel collection- my trout lures.

Remember, trout are fly-oriented. This means that a hackle tail on a small spinner is a plus. Spinners get my #1 nod and there is a great variety of makes and designs. My favourites are Helin's Rooster Tail™- 1/8 Oz. To 1/16 oz., Luhr-Jensen's Bang Tail™- same sizes, Panther Martin™- Size 2 and 4 in painted or metal designs- with or without hackle tails, and Mepps™ Size 1 to Size 00.

Please refer to my Ultralight article for a list of lures. I won't re-state everything here, but a brief run-down will save time. Suppose you could pack a hip-box of stream creatures that would be practically guaranteed to appeal to stream trout. Approach a hole in the current and cast some of the following just ahead of them. (You want the bait to drift right by their noses.)

An imitation grasshopper, cricket, crayfish, beetles, frogs, bumblebees- I like Rebel imitations- They are really life-like.

A small minnow. Rebel™, Rapala™.

A "Super Duper" A Luhr-Jensen ™ JEM! It looks like nothing else. And it works!

Acme Little Cleo™ spoon- small.

Krockodile Spoon™-small

Phoebe Spoons™- amazing action.

A Rapala Rattlin'' Shad™- a small one.

Blue Fox Spinning Minnow™- Size 1.

Dardevle Spinnie™ Spoon.

Size F7 Helin Flatfish™.

Use the same rod, reel and line mentioned in the Ultralight article and fish pools, along weed beds, and behind current obstructions like large rocks. Bonus panfish may be in the offing.

Bring a trout net, creel or stringer, measuring tape (for bragging purposes, and a cooler if you can. Respect local and provincial bag limits. Try to disturb the fishes' environment as little as possible- you're entering their world- which has been disrupted seriously in so many places. No litter.

As mentioned earlier, Brook Trout need clean, cool, oxygen rich water. Rainbow trout can survive water that is a bit warmer but remain basically a cool water fish. Brown Trout are the most adaptable of the trout and may be found in waters that are too warm for, and perhaps too dirty for, other species of trout.

If you intend to release your prize, please handle it gently- as little as possible. Use surgical pliers or needle-nose pliers. Place the fish gently in the water and give it time to revive itself. If it continually goes "belly-up" it probably won't survive so dispose of it humanely and quickly.

I'd like to say that delicate fishing with small hooks and floats really comes into its own here. Use a pencil float like a Drennan™ or Thill™. Run your line thru the top and bottom of the float and then down as far as you want to suspend your bait. Use the LIGHTEST split-shot sinkers possible (heavier in a strong current to hold the bait over the fish). Single eggs and small spawn sacks are the best. Articificals like JensenEggs™, Berkley Power Eggs™, Berkley Power Bait™, Berkley Gulp™Eggs and Mr. Twister Exude Roe ™ work very well in these situations. *Note that Power Bait™, Magnum Power Eggs™, and Gulp Eggs™ float, so you have to use weight to get them to suspend. (Please see the articles "Salmon and Trout Fall Fishing", and "Hook, Line, and Sinker", for a slip sinker rig that you can use for these baits.) I mentioned small hooks- use sizes 10-16. You don't need to go bigger. If you plan to release fish or minimize hook damage, pinch the barb with a set of pliers to make the hook barbless.

The best ways to locate trout streams, ponds, and rivers are to ask local bait store dealers, consult Ministry of Natural Resources Guidebooks, and talk to the locals. Don't be offended if someone won't reveal their own fishing spot. I wouldn't... BUT...you can at least ASK the names of streams and rivers that hold runs of trout. I'd also suggest checking listings for trout ponds. Some are very exclusive and expensive. Some are open to the public for a fee.

NOTE: <u>Have your license and watch for private property</u>.

This discussion wouldn't be complete without cleaning and cooking. A freshly caught fish should be cleaned as soon as possible and kept cool. A cooler is ideal. I like pan-frying, grilling in foil, and barbecuing trout best. The usual for me: sliced onions, salt, black pepper, a touch of garlic powder, lemon or lime squeezed over the cooked fillet. Pair with fries or fire baked potatoes. The ultimate culinary tour de force.

These are beautiful fish. Your approach should be as delicate as they are. To end with style, I quote Dame Juliana Berners, 1450A.D.

"And if the angler catches the fish with difficulty, then there is no man merrier in their spirits than he." (With apology to the Gals- Just direct quoting- I MEANT you too!!)

Outdoors Guy

Reedin' the Weeds

"Cover me, I'm goin' in!" That about sums it up if you're either a smaller fish or a larger game fish looking for some shade. Weeds serve a number of purposes. They can provide shade. They are protection for smaller fish that would prefer to avoid being seen. Naturally there are certain types of cover associated with certain fish. It wouldn't be any fun if we couldn't figure them out. Kind of like certain hoodlums relating to certain hang-outs. Let's take a look at the likely hideaways of some game fish.

Pike: These are the biggest bullies on a lot of playgrounds. Typical pike behaviour will find them either cruising weed beds where they know smaller fish are hiding, or actually hiding in the weeds themselves waiting to ambush passing prey. It makes sense that pike don't waste their time with 1 or 2 weeds. They relate to large weed beds. What you are looking for is a bed of either lily pads with accompanying cabbage and milfoil growth. The cabbage may be sub-surface. Larger weed beds may be visible from the surface. The trick is to locate an area of cover large enough to hide pike. The weeds serve as the ideal areas to track smaller fish- the more extensive the better. Lots of places for prey to try to hide, the more chances more pike will be hunting in the area. If weeds seem to pose a threat to tangle you lures, use some tricks. Spinnerbaits with long arms are weed resistant. In addition, use weedless spoons with 3 inch plastic grubs. These can be run thru and even over weeds. If you are fishing an area with submerged weeds, use a lure like a Mann's Baby 1 Minus™ or Storm Sub Wort™ to skim the top of the weeds. These baits create a wake and they rattle. Add the use of a top water lure to just skirt the edge of weed beds or fish above submerged weeds. Fish lying in wait can be enticed to hit out of hunger or anger. Don't be afraid to make some noise. If the fish are aggressive, go after them!

Largemouth Bass: Mention lily pads and images of Largemouth Bass will almost automatically come to mind. These broad-leafed weeds provide shade and oxygen. They are also ideal ambush cover for bass in search of minnows and frogs- a Largemouth staple. A key feature in the overall "map" is the availability of nearby deeper water where the fish can "drop down" into the thermocline level in summer for cooler, more oxygen-rich water. A lake that supports a healthy population of smaller bait fish/panfish must have areas for them to hide. A good rule of thumb is that smaller fish will inhabit the inside of cover, while larger fish will cruise the outside edge and weave their ways thru cover on the prowl. Larger fish know where their prey are located. If their prey know what's good for them, they won't stray far from cover.

The lures aforementioned will work very well for Largemouth Bass. Now add a Texas Rigged plastic worm to the arsenal or some bass jigs with weed guards that you can drop right into pockets and you have a formidable store of weaponry for stalking this species of fish. At this point our discussion naturally turns to the fish hiding in the weeds, trying to be inconspicuous.

Perch, Sunfish, Crappies, Rock Bass: Confined to smaller quarters, these fish nevertheless have their own share of smaller creatures to feed on. As long as they can avoid detection from predators they're OK. Small jigs, imitation creature lures like frogs, grasshoppers, minnows, and crayfish are effective. The twitching minnow technique mentioned in the micro-light article comes into its own here. The vegetation around a weed bed may not be more than a few feet deep. Casting a minnow out, twitching it so that it dives a foot or 2, then allowing it to struggle back up to the surface like a crippled baitfish is a good way to get close to smaller game fish in deep weed cover. Small top water lures fished near weed beds can lure fish. My experience has been that they are more likely to extend their range in the early morning or late evening- when they aren't in "broad daylight". Smaller game fish will venture out of their protection only so far. Their instinct for protection is very strong. They KNOW that they can't stray far from protective cover. Example: Crappies will come out to investigate a small crippled minnow lure. But they won't KEEP following it out into open water. They just know better than to do that. So if you find they've stopped following, reel in and cast in closer again. I've seen Rock Bass behave in a similar fashion. They'll follow a surface lure to a point away from their weed cover or rock pile, then return to cover.

*Again, it should be noted that traveling in a school is a common Crappie strategy for safety. They are often found in and close to bull rushes and downed timber in the branches, but they also travel widely. So don't always rely on weeds close to shore. The Crappies may be out roaming in a school. During the day they are likely down, somewhere at the thermocline level. Then, using a side-finder sonar is the best way to locate them.

I may guess some readers are wondering what happened to Smallmouth Bass. I wouldn't forget them! I would like to point out that half of a Smallmouth's diet is soft-shelled crayfish. This crustacean hides in rocks. Therefore Smallmouth invest proportionally more time foraging around rocks than they do weeds. Having said that, it ISN'T a hard and fast rule! You will often find Smallmouth Bass in the same areas you find Largemouth Bass. They eat a lot of the same forage- frogs, minnows, etc. Top water lures, spinners, 3 inch grubs and jigs, minnows and crank baits are equally welcomed by both species. The difference is the balance of time spent by one species in a specific area is different from the other species. It's a relative situation, not an either/or.

The beginning angler really knows their stuff all right! Most youngsters use a spin-cast rod and bobber/worm combination and cast this set-up into the (you guessed it) weeds! Where else would perch and sunfish be hanging out? Just add a few years- and some increased knowledge and experience- and you have an expanded picture of different species of fish relating to weeds in their respective ways. Combine that knowledge with the need for adjacent deeper water, times of day, types of lures/

presentations to use to catch them, and the preferences of certain species for certain types of weeds, then you're still a kid at heart, but with a glint in your eye that says, "I've learned a few things since those days."

I would also like to suggest that submerged growth large enough to hold a quantity of fish may only be spotted by a sonar unit. It's worth considering buying even a portable, battery-operated one. They can show you a whole new underwater world.

Keep That Learning Always Happening- Then You Can Pass It On!

Outdoors Guy

Outdoors Guy- Salmon and Trout Fall Fishing

I happen to live in one those favoured areas which features a salmon and trout run in the Fall. Oh Most Fortunate of Mortals! This is the Double Rewards Miles for fisher-folk.

I look back at how I started Fall fishing for Chinooks and smile. A tempered steel rod about 4 feet long, 20lb. Test line, and even using spinner baits and bass poppers. Give a little slack. This was 30 years ago. If I haven't learned anything since that time, I'm really not capable of learning much of anything at any time.

The stock-in-trade equipment for Fall salmon fishing is the noodle rod. The brain child of Canadian Lorne Greene, this gave salmon fishers the tool they needed. Sporting lengths of 9 ½ ft. to 14 ½ ft., this amazing invention allows the use of much lighter lines than could previously have been possible.

With salmon and trout, fishing in clear waters, every advantage someone can get is a must. Using 20lb. Line, "In case I get a BIG one on!" is amusing. This line is very visible to the fish (and is stiff enough to seriously limit your casting distance). I DID have a big one on with 20lb. Line, ONCE, and the fish took off and snapped the line like it was thread!

A noodle rod is long and slender with the idea that you pressure a running fish relatively more with the ROD rather than with the LINE. I use 8lb. Test (NO higher than 10lb.) for Chinook fishing in the Fall. I have a 10 ½ ft. Ugly Stik™ and I also have an 11 ½ ft. noodle rod as well.

A noodle rod is extremely flexible so as to absorb at lot of the stress which would otherwise be added to your line. Understand that a salmon (or large trout) when it returns to spawn, is a powerful fish, having reached adult size. With this in mind, the noodle rod is again the choice. Fighting a salmon isn't a matter of "horsing" the fish, as you can do steering a large bass out of cover. A salmon has to tire out which means, in most instances, a prolonged, stubborn battle. The noodle rod was designed to wear the fish down gradually and to allow it to run- which is what it has to do to become tired. Be PATIENT! A large fish takes time to wear out. Enjoy the sport. When the fish comes progressively closer to shore or the edge of the pier and starts making only short, furtive runs, it's getting close to the end of its energy. Try to net the fish as soon as you can if you plan to take a photo and release it. It wants to swim away and recover.

Noodle rods can very pricey. Not knocking that. The top end rods are made by companies with a long standing reputation for quality and excellence in design. I just happen to live on a budget. Even though you can't afford the best, buy the best you CAN afford. There's far less of an argument in support of buying junk. Give yourself the tools to work with. Many medium priced rods will do the job quite respectably. Shop the outdoor stores and look for the sales. Ask the clerks questions. A rod may be from an obsolete line but be very reliable.

Reels should have a large spool capacity. It isn't unheard of for a large salmon to "spool" someone. They make a long, determined run and strip off ALL the line. No drag left and no rod leverage left= line snaps.

Reliable reels have several ball bearings and a smooth, reliable drag system. The brand names have been around and are going to stay around because they mean good quality. I sincerely believe that in fishing, as in every other business, people don't mind paying good money if they know they're getting QUALITY. Shimano™, Abu Garcia™, and Daiwa™ have earned their reputation. Stick with the proven brands. I use a 20 series reel although a 30 series is a good choice. Because of the noodle rod, I can use 8lb. test and get away with it. Using lighter line means you can spool more of it onto your reel, which gives you more playing distance when the fish signals that they're taking off.

Good quality line is a MUST! There is nothing like wasting money on a bargain. The line doesn't have the shock strength, flexibility, knot strength, or break strength to do the job. You'll be left waiting until the store opens again before you get another chance to land a fish. I stick with Berkely Trilene Big Game™. It is what its name implies. This line is strong and stands the strain of a fight. I also favour Cabelas' Pro Line™ and Bass Pro's Excel™. These lines are smooth, limp, castable, and strong.

Now we're getting down to it… from large to small. And small is equally important. We have to discuss the fine points- lures, hooks, leaders, knots, baits.

Fine wire "salmon hooks" are stronger than they look. I suggest either black or "steelhead red" hooks. Gamakatsu™, Mustad™, VMC™, and Eagle Claw™ are reliable brands. They have been pre-sharpened at the factory. Hooks must be more than needle sharp. As a test, run the point of a hook LIGHTLY over a fingernail. It should leave a small groove easily. Another way to describe a properly sharpened hook is that is "sticky sharp" when handled (carefully). Sizes in 6-12 are best.

Knots are the point of sale in a bait rig. I use a Trilene Knot™- 2 loops thru the hook eye, 6 turns around the line, then feed the working end of the line thru the double loops. Moisten the knot with saliva and draw tight. Snelling bait hooks is excellent. Simple snell knots can easily be found online NOTE: Re-tie occasionally. Any knot can weaken over time. I lost a beautiful rainbow after just having landed a salmon. Reason- weakened knot from having fought the last fish.

My bait "rig" if you will, is simple. I feed the main line thru an egg shaped sinker and tie the end onto a swivel. The leader line is tied onto the other end of the swivel. 10lb. main line and 8lb. leader for salmon. The leader should be no more than 9 inches to a foot off bottom. Fish will be looking for eggs to eat which will be on bottom. Higher up isn't natural to them.

If you are fishing in a current or there are weeds or branches (or whatever) on bottom, use a float- basically the same principle as an egg-sinker rig- to get the bait down to where the fish are feeding.

Use a tapered float and NOT the old red and white bobber we used as kids to catch sunfish with a hook and worm. Why? Fish have to sense/feel as little resistance to their bite as possible. A float should just be able to maintain its position on top of the water and submerge with very little pressure from the fish. My choice for floats is a tapered float that you can thread a line right thru from top to bottom. Adding split shot to the leader end of the line should be judged by how fast a current may be moving. Use the lightest split shot possible and attach it at intervals of 6 inches to a foot along the leader line. Try to determine the depth of the bottom and then adjust the length of the leader as you search for the fish.

Without a doubt, the top bait for salmon and trout is roe. I believe that if the fish are going to hit natural bait, they'll hit roe quickly. To preserve, wash roe thoroughly for a few minutes in cold water. Spread out on a paper towel and let dry for 15 minutes. Then wrap in small freezer bags- each the right size for a day's or night's fishing. Preserving roe by using borax or curing in a commercially available mix- Pro Cure™, will allow your eggs to last longer when thawed out. Pro-Cure™ gives the roe a deep colour that is attractive to fish.

Tie 5 or 6 eggs in spawn netting and add the same number of egg sac floaters (tiny Styrofoam pellets used to float an egg sac). I use Red Wing Spider Thread™ to tie off my roe bags.

Pop 1 egg in the egg sac when putting it on the hook. Cast, and relax and have a coffee from the thermos.

There are plenty of other ways to use bait. Marshmallows (the store bought kind and also commercially available special salmon and trout marshmallows in delectable flavours like shrimp, cheese, and garlic) are effective. Marshmallows don't last long, so re- bait regularly. I have used Berkley Gulp Eggs™ and Power Eggs™ with success. Luhr Jensen's Jensen Eggs™ are a good substitute when float fishing. These egg imitations seem to work more effectively for trout than they do for salmon.

My top choices for lures are: 1. A Flatfish™ in a fluorescent co-lour (many fisher-individuals swear by red in the Fall and green in the Spring), Vibrating lipless crank baits, large Rapala™, Bomber™, or Rebel™ minnows, and spoons (Acme Little Cleos™and Krocodile-Luhr Jensen™), and fluorescent Mepps™ spinners from sizes #3 to #5.

Probably the best way to learn is to talk to the locals. Find out where the runs and the best pools are (if they'll tell you that is...). There are so many tips and techniques. Don't forget that trout and some Coho salmon run in the spring.

Oh to live near a salmon and trout run river. The above mentioned are my preferred and suggested methods- lots more to learn. Hope you come home with that BIG fish and a grin a mile wide. Tight Lines!

*I have a bonus for you in this article. Please turn the page to see how to construct your own rod stand for bait fishing. The PVC pipe should be roughly twice the diameter of your rod handle.

Hang On!! These fish will give you the Fight of the Century. Excitement spelled S-A-L-M-O-N!

Basic Egg Sac Rig for Fishing With Roe:
Several eggs tied in a spawn sac with 1 floater per egg. The
sac is commercial netting tied into a small sac about the size
of a dime. Run the hook (salmon hook- size 6-12) thru one edge
of the egg sac. Pop one egg to release scent and cast out. The
roe sac is suspendedabout 9" from the bottom.

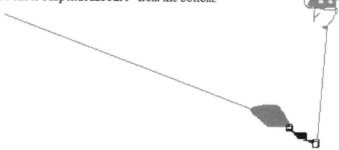

Basic Rod Stand Design: Materials: 16" black PVC pipe, 2 16" 2 x 4's and 1 12
x 18 inch base board. Cut PVC pipe at a 45 degree angle, top and bottom,
about 12" to 15". Nail the baseboard to the cross pieces to form the base.
Drill 3 holes into the PVC near the base and screw it onto the base with 3
strong screws. To avoid problems, the screws should be completely
embedded into the rear cross piece. Voila! Simple and stable.

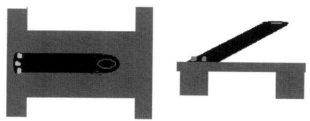

Outdoors Guy...Carps!!

This edition of Outdoors Guy is dedicated to a very special
friend. I met Old John about 27 years ago in Bronte Harbour. He
was fighting an enormous fish. I asked him what he was fishing
for and he answered, "Carps!"

Fishing

John had survived the Gulags after the war- at one point escaping a labour camp and travelling 1 000 miles on foot, (with only an improvised knife), only to be returned. He was innately very smart and resourceful. I enjoyed hearing him tell stories about his life. He migrated to Canada and worked his way up to Foreman at Oakville's Procor tank car plant. His fellows bought him, you guessed it, a fishing rod for retirement. He was fascinating. John was a master fisherman. And thanks to him, another venue of my own fishing opened up.

The carp is looked at as a trash fish by some people. I don't believe that this reputation is entirely fair. A carp can adapt to waters that practically every other species would find unsuitable. It's not that they deliberately CHOOSE dirty, warm water. They can survive in it.

Not that carp are the loveliest creatures (if beauty is in the eye of the beholder- go catch a carp and judge for yourself). They have a sucker-like mouth and feed on minnows, crustaceans and decaying material on the bottom of lakes and rivers. Orange and brown in colour, this fish can reach a gigantic size. To give a balanced perspective on carp, there are specialty clubs in the UK that devote themselves to catching carp and they take pride in choosing their tackle and baits. Carp are commercially raised as a delicacy in farm ponds in China. If you go out to dinner at an Oriental restaurant and see a gold fish pond, look for the larger species with sucker lips. They are members of the carp family. (As proof of this fish's resilience, I went fishing in Bronte once in a shallow cove and found a member of the carp family- a 3-4 lb…goldfish! How it got there, don't ask. I don't know…but what a survivor.)

Carp are a powerful fish. They won't exhibit the aerial acrobatics of Bass. More like a big Brown Trout, they slug it out subsurface. You need medium heavy to heavy equipment to handle carp and a smooth, dependable reel with ample spool capacity. These fish take off on long, determined runs that rate with mature salmon. If your drag is too tight, or you have old line, they'll likely take off and snap the line. They can make it look easy. Expect a prolonged, stubborn battle with carp. They are terrific fun. A typical battle can last upwards of ½ an hour.

As mentioned, strong gear is needed to handle these fish. A noodle rod (mentioned in the Salmon article) is a good choice for lighter (say 8 lb.) line. Other than that, medium heavy spinning gear or bait casting gear are the order of the day. Rods around 7-7 ½ ft. with plenty of backbone are the ticket. Line 8 lb. to 12 lb.

Bait for carp and how to "rig it" is simple. Simply tie a Size 4 or size 2 hook onto your line and use the top bait- dough balls you make by yourself . The easiest way is to buy the freshest, gooiest white bread you can find, roll the dough into balls the size of a quarter, mould one on you hook and cast. Let the dough sink to the bottom and leave it there. Have a coffee and chill. Leave a bit of hook exposed for setting it when a carp bites.

If you want something really enticing to lure carp, here's Outdoors Guy's "Top Secret Recipe" (as if)! Use corn meal and bring water to a boil in a saucepan. When you add the cornmeal, stir frequently and turn the heat down to simmer. It is exactly like making oatmeal of Cream of Wheat or Red River Cereal (which can also be used). After the meal has absorbed the water, the trick is to add corn starch and stir until the dough stiffens- much like thickening gravy. The dough should have the same consistency as the white bread balls- it has to be able to stay on the hook. It takes a little practice to get the dough the right consistency. Best to add and combine ingredients slowly rather than ruining a whole batch. If you can pick up the dough when cooled and make it into a ball that will stick on your hook and stay there, good work! Lots of corn starch, progressively added, is the trick. (Now…for the secret "in-greedy-ent"…Add a dash of vanilla and/or table syrup to the mix. Carp really like it.)

Carp will frequent muddy waters with rocky bottoms. Rocks serve as a cover for crayfish which are a staple in the carp's diet. I suggest checking Ontario Fishing books published by the Ministry of Natural Resources and/or ask the locals. Peterborough's lock system was renowned for carp at one time for carp. But my knowledge is based on my parents' recollections a long time ago. I've always fishing Bronte Harbour in West Oakville. You just have to know where the carp waters are. I've never seen Pike or Bass bite dough balls- these a a <u>carp</u> specialty!

You can add a sinker a few feet ahead of the dough ball. The bait should sink. Carp are bottom feeders. Trust me, when the carp takes your bait- you'll know it!! Have your rod anchored in a good rod stand or well braced. The carp can easily just take off with all your stuff.

As mentioned, prepare for the Fight of the Century if you hook a big carp. Besides being strong, they have a great deal of endurance. The fight alone is worth it!! Have a LARGE NET on hand. When the carp is tiring, keep the pressure on. When you land it can almost guarantee you'll have this silly grin and a feeling of immense satisfaction at having handled a monster and having landed it successfully. The question you may well ask yourself next is, "OK, now what do I DO with it?" John said that smoked carp, processed properly, is very fine eating. Why not snap a photo and return the fish? I just release mine after having said thank you for the fun. (No goodbye kisses- these fish ARE no Miss Universe…)

I know that the plural of "carp" is, "carp". I don't care. To me they'll always be "carps". This article is dedicated to you, John- My Friend.

Outdoors Guy

Out Doors Guy On Ice

Six or seven months is a long time between fishing trips. It's freezing out there, but the fish are somewhere down there in the depths. Maybe you'd be interested in trying ice fishing. The best way to catch ice is in an ice cube tray. Ok. I'll stop. I really did mean getting out there on a lake and seeking out some fish. It can be a lot of fun but practical me says that this is winter and of course not so climatically friendly. Some practical advice is in order.

First- dress warmly!! I love my Russian hat, Khrushchev. He helps me fight the "Cold War!" (Couldn't resist this one.) My ears are well covered. The trick for winter clothing really is…layers. Air in a dead air space is an insulator. Several layers will serve you better than 1 thick layer. Also remember that the majority of body heat can be lost thru your hands, feet and head. Hands and feet are primary frostbite targets and must be well covered. Cold feet can make an ice fishing trip MISERABLE. There are gloves commercially available that are waterproof that are handy (no pun) for situations like hauling in a fish, scooping slush out of an ice hole, etc. Look for the temperature rating on boots and wear 2 layers of socks, 1 your normal socks, the 2nd layer warmer insulating socks. Again, layers.

With all this extra clothing on it's reasonable to think about safety. Humans aren't as buoyant in freezing water, and if you go in you have a LOT of soaking wet extra weight working against you if you're trying to stay above water and get back onto the ice. So here's some safety thoughts. I personally cheat. I'll wait until I see plenty of other fisher-type people on the ice. Might as well let them test it out for me first! This is a good indication of the ice's ability to support weight.

Next, do some research. Find out from local stores, websites, MNR officials, etc. what the ice conditions are. Generally, and I'm a coward, 1-3 inches...ABSOLUTELY NOT!!!! 4 inches, light general use. 6 inches+ =safe. Don't risk it. Play safe and make sure first. Testing the ice by just blindly wandering out to see if it's safe enough is dangerous.

Some other considerations which are important are environmental factors like wind and bright sunlight. We know it's cold and we've dressed for that. Wind can be nasty, not only whipping snow in your face which will cause frostbite, but also causing wind burn. One idea is use Vaseline to protect your face. It works. You can also think of a scarf over your face or wearing a balaclava.

Sun on bright snow and ice can cause temporary snow blindness after long exposure- a GOOD pair of UV sun glasses are in order here.

There are some excellent ice-fishing shelters available which come set up like a sled or toboggan. They can cover you from 3 sides, and some come with enclosures. You can cut a couple of ice holes, then pull the shelter over them. Be careful of strong winds. I personally think it's far safer to go out on calm, sunny days. Check on weather conditions from time to time if you're in an ice hut. If conditions are worsening, i.e. wind whipping up, blowing snow, getting darker, best to pack up rather than face steadily worsening conditions.

Chopping a hole in the ice is hard work with an axe (I've also used a crowbar sharpened at one end). A hand or power auger is a good investment if you can afford one- and MUCH less effort. The blades usually come in 6",7", and 8" sizes, so it would make sense before you purchase to consider what species of fish you're going out after. Smaller fish like perch can easily be pulled up thru a 6" ice hole. But if you're after larger game, consider at least the 7" auger. You need to haul the larger fish up thru the ice with a gaff, and their girth has to squeeze thru the opening. Again, you can work smarter in some instances. I look for newly vacated ice holes and re-open them. It's far less work. Also, checking out previously opened ice holes will give you an accurate idea of the depth of the ice. A trick I've used to improvise a gaff is to take a broom handle (wood) and then get a large double-pronged hook (like those used on rubber frogs for bass) and screw it into the handle with the hooks protruding from the end. Tape it with electrician's tape for added strength and wind some tape around the handle.. Finally, add an ice scoop to the set of gear for keeping the ice hole open and clear.

Warmth must remain a concern. The "Hobo Stove" I talked about way back when deserves to be called back to mind here. A large coffee can with briquettes and holes punched in the bottom to provide air flow can be kept glowing for hours. It's light and well worth that little extra carrying space. Place about a half inch of sand on the bottom and some brown paper (like the LCBO bags). Place the coals on top and light. The coals have to get started, so persist. Once this is going, however, you can add a few coals at a time and the warmth is wonderful for chilled hands. (*Please refer to Article #2 for a diagram.)

My favourite way to fish is with 2 ice rods- one baited with eggs and a float, the other for jigging with a spoon or lure. These rods may look strange to a person who's never seen them before, a person used to 6-7ft. rods for the summer. The idea is that you have very little room for that rod to bend if you're fishing thru a small ice hole. So these rods fit the bill perfectly. My largest fish was a 16lb. Rainbow and I landed it with an ice rod approximately 18 inches long. Don't worry! They get the job done. It may also be noted that cold water actually makes monofilament line stronger. But use new line. Chalky looking line with a dull powdery finish is no good so start with fresh, premium quality line. (Again, I unabashedly give Trilene Big Game™ the overwhelming nod). As a rule of thumb- smaller fish, 6 lb. line. General use for walleyes, bass, average sized pike, 8 lb. line. For larger fish- 10 lb. or 12 lb. limp line. Remember, heavy line can be seen, and can stiffen up into coils in cold water. Try to use the lightest lb. test you think you can comfortably get away with.

So with an ice rod you can drop live bait like minnows, real or artificial eggs (there are some excellent artificial eggs out there now, Berkeley GULP™ floating eggs, Mister Twister Exude Eggs™, and Berkeley Power Eggs™ are my favourites. And yes, I have caught fish with them.

Using spoons like a Williams Wabler™ which flutter and give an excellent imitation of a swimming minnow is highly effective. Test several depths. I usually let the spoon drop until I see the line go slack- it's now on bottom. Reel in about a foot of line and then jig the spoon erratically. Try a few longer sweeps, then a few shorter sweeps. Let the spoon flutter. You may have to try this at different depths to see where fish may be holding. Some spoons for bass are very heavy and get down fast. My own personal preference is for lighter spoons that flutter.

There is a wide variety of great ice lures like Rapala's Jigging Shad Rap™, Swedish Pimple™, tear drop jigs tipped with bait, normal "walleye-sized" jigs tipped with minnows. Hang around at the local tackle store, talk to the other fishermen and ask a few questions. Again, do a little research. What is this lake known for? Perch? Pike? Whitefish? Lake Trout? Local store owners are often very knowledgeable and friendly and consider it part of their job to have good advice. Never hurts to ask. General rule of thumb: smaller minnows- perch. Up to 4-6 inch chub or sucker minnows for pike. Tip: Hooking a small minnow thru the tail fin or back allows it to swim more freely. It can breathe better because it can open its mouth easier. You can add a trailer (or "stinger") hook for larger minnows

Finally, within the scope of this article, we can consider the use of a tip-up. This handy device allows you to drop bait into a hole and then watch while you actively fish close by thru another hole. It has 2 cross bars which spread out along the ice over the hole. Use the lightest sinkers possible. The really great part is next. These devices come with a flag that you fold over along the upright pole of the tip-up. When a fish takes the bait, the flag is released and you can SEE it. The fun starts when you grab the hand line and pull the fish thru the ice before it gets any bright ideas about taking off. It is very effective for smaller trout and whitefish. With a larger game fish, remember, this ISN'T a fishing rod, so...good luck.

Consider going out with some friends. Alone isn't an idea if no one else is around. In the event of a mishap, you need friends. Take a guy rope with you and anchor it to something solid like a mooring bracket for a boat, dock piling, tree...anything. You'll stand a better chance if you can pull yourself up flat onto the ice than you would be just flailing your arms. Carry some long nails in your pocket to help grip the ice. But best really is to make sure the ice is so solid that these accidents won't happen. Avoid suspicious looking black ice. Better to be live coward than a dead (frozen) duck. If you feel ice below you weakening, lie flat on the ice to distribute your weight and pull yourself to a safer location. This shouldn't happen if you've made sure you're standing on firm ice in the first place. MAKE SURE FIRST!!

Plan ahead and go out for a few hours. Leave the ice before it gets dark. Tell someone where you are. Carry a cell phone. This sport can be so much fun, especially with a few friends to yak with, a thermos of hot coffee, and the occasional fish. Please... bop the fish on the head instead of just leaving it lying there. Be humane.

Being stuck inside for 6-7 months is no fun. This sport allows you to get outside and appreciate nature's beauty- winter style. Please be safe, do your preparation ahead of time. This is one sport where you CAN fish with 2 rods. They have to be no more than 60ft. away from each other. Ministry of Natural Resources has several excellent booklets you can get for free on fish populations in local lakes, plus valuable information on regulations. 1 final tip…have your license current and in your pocket.

I know I've said it before, but…**PLEASE BE SAFE**- especially with this kind of fishing. Plan to take all the right gear and safety precautions. Maybe you'll discover a whole new type of fishing and then you can listen to people say, "Going ice-fishing? You must be crazy!" Crazy, if you haven't prepared, but can be a lot of fun if you have. You may discover a new hobby. Pick a nice, sunny, clear, bright happy day and try going out for an hour or 2. Guaranteed people won't think you're abnormal, any more than anyone who fishes at ANY time of the year is abnormal…

Your Pal,

Outdoors Guy

Tackle Storage- Just a Little Care Makes So Much Difference

The equipment is being stored for the winter. The way it's put down will be how it's picked up. This sounds so simple, yet think about it... You'd like to begin next season ready to go. There are some important tackle care items to attend to that will help open next season with everything ready and in great shape. Maybe more than you'd think at first. In no set order, here are a few practical considerations and tasks that won't take long, but will make a difference next spring.

Line- Line that has been used for a few seasons (maybe even one season) should be replaced. Now if you really want to go on the cheap, here's a money-saving tip. If you have 2 spinning reels take the line off of one reel. Then wind the line off of the other reel. The "back half" of the line you're winding off should be in newer condition. This presumes that a fish hasn't routinely stripped, say 150 yards of line on a run last summer. It also presumes that the line on the feeder reel hasn't been left for years and is so stiff and chalky (a sign of deteriorated line) that is all useless and is best just thrown away.

No matter, you should always start each season with fresh, new line on each reel, spooled to within 1/8 inch from the reel's full capacity. Again (nag, nag, NAG!!!), use premium quality line. Bargain basement line is sold at bargain basement prices for a reason.

Where rods and reels are stored can make quite a difference. Not-so-good places include: out in the back shed, anywhere where there's gas, paint solvents, or heat (so not right beside a heating vent) or where it's just cold all winter. I store my equipment in its own quiet corner in the house, out of the line of UV rays, which damage line over time. My spare line is kept in a cool place- usually in the freezer. Store gear in dry, dark, cool, and clean places.

Reels need to be maintained so why not set that task aside for a time when you're just sitting and have some spare time during the winter. Begin by removing the reel handle and then the side plate. Have a fine screwdriver on hand for this. Clean out any dirt (especially sand which can chew moving parts in a reel to pieces). Spraying WD-40 on the moving parts can help clean them. Remove as much dirt, grit, and old grease as you can. Dry the inside by wiping with a paper towel and then pack the moving parts with fresh grease. Replace the plate and handle. Make sure none of the oil or grease came into contact with your line. Next remove the spool by unscrewing the drag button (if the reel has a front drag system). Clean as before and replace. Note: line on a spinning reel can often get caught under the under the spool and will have grease on it. Cut it off and discard. *Note, this paragraph uses the terms generally related to spinning reels, but the same idea applies to spin cast reels and bait cast reels. If you own a fancy bait caster and are concerned about gears slipping, etc., maybe a trip to the tackle store would be better. I'm more familiar with the intricacies of spinning reels.

Check the bail spring and anti-reverse by opening the bail and reeling. A weak bail spring will not close the bail consistently. It is possible to replace a bail spring by using a hook hanger from a Flatfish or by cutting and bending the arms from a small safety pin. It's one of the easier home repairs you can make, usually. Check the anti-reverse lever simply by opening then closing the bail and then pull line off the reel through the bail. If the anti-reverse is set, the line should stop and the drag system should kick in.

Finally, loosen the drag off completely and leave it that way until spring. Tightly compressed washers and discs can start to corrode and or stick together making the drag system ineffective next year. Typical of this situation is a drag jamming or releasing line erratically instead of smoothly. Back the drag off. It should be said that cheaply made drag systems are, well, cheaply made and no amount of loosening will make much difference, overall. As stated before, buy the best you can afford. Then take care of that good drag system. It's designed to give you years of enjoyment if you maintain it properly.

Rods should be checked for small nicks and tiny sharp edges inside rod line guides. Look for weaknesses caused by UV rays. Store them <u>inside</u> and not out "in the shed".

Lures and lure boxes may contain unexpected surprises in the spring. A big no-no is leaving soft plastic baits piled up, or at least in contact with hard plastic baits. Give it all winter and then you'll see why this was careless. Soft plastics will actually eat into and dissolve paint finishes and the plastic itself in hard lures. (Ok, yes...I've made this mistake.)

The tackle box was open and got wet in the rain last day of the season. Not thinking much of it, our hero puts it away for the Winter and opens it to find rusted hooks and, as a bonus, rust all over their lures. Even a bit of water left on the lure trays can bring about this undesirable consequence. If there's water in your tackle box, take the contents out (carefully, mind you) and dry them off with a paper towel, especially the lure compartments. Thus, dry and clean you can store your treasures for next season. (I always take them out and admire them in the winter. Who can ignore gems in a box for 6 straight months?) By the way, if you have lures with hooks that are rusted, clean them or replace them. They'll either break and you'll lose a fish and/or cause disease when the rust penetrates the fish's mouth or when you make a mistake and the hook penetrates YOUR skin. As a last tip, if you've got lures tangled up like a crazed mob, take them out, sort them out, and put them back in order. Almost everyone has left a nest in their tackle boxes, but sort them out now. You may find that you have too many lures for THIS tackle box...which totally justifies you going to the Tackle Store and buying a new one. (We fisher-people are excellent cons when it comes to plausible excuses to go buy...)

Same deal for paddles, life jackets, rope, fish stringers, nets. All dry. Nets should be rinsed before drying, especially if they've been handling pike slime. They'll SMELL better in the spring.

Same advisory against paint and gas fumes. Clean and dry. Your canoe should at least be elevated and not just lying on the ground. You want to preserve the foam bumpers as long as you can.

This isn't a long article. With only a little care you can keep your equipment stored in good condition and you'll thank yourself in the spring. You invested good money in a sport you love. With that love goes some care. Attention to some important details. Imagine…well-oiled and greased reels (a.k.a. smooth operating- like they were out of the store box), drag working properly, new line, lures all sorted out and ready to go. In short, no last minute cleaning, fixing and gritted teeth over damaged equipment. Go get 'em, Champ!!! See you in the spring!

Outdoors Guy

Survival

Outdoors Guy- Surviving- Using Your Emotions To Help You

This issue is going to be different than anything I've written, or am likely to write again. It's a product of evening reflection on survival and just basic human needs. It struck me that the links between the 2 are strong and related to something not just topical. We exist/live/survive with hard-wired minds and spirits which demand that certain things be "right" in our world. The lack of these needs is sharply accentuated in a true survival situation. All of a sudden, things aren't "right" anymore. Something's happened we didn't expect. We can panic, or calmly look at the immediate situation and begin to think of how to start making the situation BETTER. Whatever has happened- HAS HAPPENED. The whole issue is, "What now?" Regret can leave you stuck. It won't change anything. The mirrors in a car have a lesson here. Looking in the rear view mirror is only a short-term necessity. Looking in it for the majority of time will cause a wreck. Being out in the wild in an emergency parallels this analogy. You may have made a mistake or over-looked something that contributed to the current situa- tion- but forget it! What matters is NOW! A situation that's bad can even become worse. You've got to make it BETTER. Stem the damage and start doing something that will help you and others.

We need to feel optimistic about our current situation and short-term future. Things are looking bright and the future has some happy moments ahead. We need regular doses of uplifts and positives- it's who we are. In a survival situation feeling overwhelmed, despondent and helpless is right at the door. It isn't about perfect in this situation. It's about anything that will make it BETTER. Having a secure shelter, enough water, warmth and a plan make things feel much better. Usually, it'll be accumulation of little things accomplished in steady doses.

We need to feel in control of our lives- in this case- of the situation. Being at the mercy of circumstances makes us helpless and ineffective. It cannot be over-stated: You are NOT helpless. You CAN have a plan. You can plan ahead, learn skills and strategies, have the right equipment. The most important feeling to boost all other feelings is: EMPOWERMENT. You ARE capable. You CAN develop a plan, and TAKE ACTION. I've had the feeling in life that things were out of place. I suspect we all have. It is easy to stay stationery and give up. You feel depressed, panicked. The only cure is to let those emotions go. Cry, do what you have to, but then get up and get going.

Assess the situation and develop a plan FIRST. Sounds silly, doesn't it? You need to act and first you sit down? Think of it this way. You can WASTE time on useless running around or you can think calmly (my brain works MUCH more effectively on this level) and develop a plan based on the factors in your situation and use your time efficiently.

We need to feel competent and capable. I'll repeat it: YES, YOU **CAN**! Believe it.

Life begs and demands that we are not only in control but have a DIRECTION. So assess the situation realistically. It isn't easy. It isn't impossible. It's a stiff challenge. It will demand probably more of your mental emotional and spiritual resources than you've had to use- maybe ever. So the ticket is first of all to ASSESS. No strategic plan ever worked without an accurate assessment of the current situation. What do you have current- ly, "in-stock"? What are the short-term and longer term goals? Using this thinking will keep you channelled and focused. Set a plan to address immediate priorities, once you have established what they are. Now... start moving! Companies have strategic plans. It's a strategy that works.

Does anyone need first aid? Can you signal another ve- hicle, phone, text, make the immediate scene safe (gas, glass fire, wire). Give yourself some decent trump cards to play! Pack that first aid kit. Learn first aid. Have a roadside kit. Have a cell phone-CHARGED.

Take stock of provisions. Hopefully you'll have some decent tools to work with- a bush knife and space blanket (critical). Water and some power bars, a flashlight, and some spare clothes-warm in winter- but also consider that you have to keep DRY as well as warm.

Next month's article focuses on essential equipment being packed into the smallest space. Efficiency. I want to bridge it by focusing on the idea of fundamental needs. Warmth, shelter from the elements, water, food, ability to communicate, safety, awareness of your location and feeling secure and safe in your immediate circumstances. Based on priorities, you develop a list of equipment. *You also have to take stock of what your immediate surroundings may be able to supplement for you. If there are branches in profusion, rocks, and a relatively safe site is close by, it means you have a base and materials for a shelter and fire.

So we get to the stage where we the initial feeling of crisis has passed. The stress of the situation hasn't, but you feel at least that you are moving in a positive direction. Having addressed the issue of empowering yourself with having equipment, skills and knowledge we come to another important human need- action. Inactivity is a breeding bed for boredom and frustration- just like a swamp is to mosquitoes. Important here is to establish what the first priority is. If all things for the moment are safe and under control, what to do next? My suggestion would be shelter. Weather may change, or it may be that you're in bad weather and it's important to improve your situation by putting some distance between yourself and the elements. First line gear would be warm clothing, mosquito netting, a rain suit. Then you have to think about what to piece together. Can you rig a tent with a tarp? Can you lay bedding down in the form of dry leaves (watch out for snakes and insects) and/or spruce boughs? Can you build a fire pit and start a fire? Is everyone involved in an orderly plan with well-defined tasks? Or, if you're by yourself, are your short-term objectives being accomplished step by step? Stop and reassess frequently to tweak your plan- then keep going.

All of us need to feel we are capable and have done a good job. We fly by our self-esteem. Feeling confident and capable is one end. Feeling a sense of pride at having done a good job of keeping a calm head, assessing accurately, planning effectively, and working efficiently are worth a self-pat on the back. Looking at something you have just created gives a sense of pride and accomplishment. There's nothing wrong with a pat on the back if you deserve it! In this situation YOU are the "Boss". (Nothing better than a pat on the back from the Boss!)

An important "next" item- we need to have a long term goal. (Of course, you want to be rescued or spotted and get home.) The situation, as long as it lasts, will be a work in progress. Situations will change. With short term priorities addressed, there's the focus on longer term. A camp can always be improved, made safer and more comfortable. We need to KEEP moving effectively. Any home (as irritating as it gets for the average home owner) needs maintenance. Homes are "upgraded". But we need to keep purposefully occupied. We need to keep thinking and assessing and planning and working.

For the moment, like any person in any life, we need that feeling that we have a safe haven, that immediate circumstances are under control- that WE are in control- that our surroundings are secure and we have enough or can get enough for immediate future. An idea may be to think this way: we need to put as much distance as we can between ourselves and the line where circumstances become critical. Enough water for the next week and enough to eat for the next few days, a shelter that will protect us from the elements and provide a place to sleep and store our gear.

If I may offer this homey suggestion: Envision what a home is like and what psychological needs it fulfills for you: comfortable, well-constructed, safe, a shelter from the elements, roomy enough, water and food readily available, a place for new projects, something to feel proud of, and a nice fire going. A shelter isn't far off this mark. Fire and a secure shelter can do so much- bed, protection from the elements, relative comfort inside. Like they say, "It ain't much, but it's home." It can provide a sense that home is safe and that the current situation is in hand. Every psychological boost helps. Having a feeling of, "at home" can be comforting.

One last thought. We all need love and fellowship. Having a plan and well defined tasks helps with 2 or more people. It's a great feeling to be working together purposefully for a common goal. I like working by myself and being in charge of developing my own ideas. But this has its drawbacks… You may just be ALONE. Keeping occupied is likely the best solution. Time to "dwell on things" could be fatal. If you've worked hard and are tired, you can sleep instead of just sitting awake and at the mercy of depression, panic, boredom, frustration, helplessness. Prayer, meditation and reflection all help us focus and maintain the will to live. The thought of beating this challenge and seeing someone we love is motivating. As kids we had an imaginary friend. I really don't think it's a bad idea! Who's going to know anyway? Why not adopt a pet? (I'd suggest staying away from rattlesnakes owing to the inherent risks…) We all need someone to bounce ideas off of. By the way- I wouldn't take this TOO far…if you're imagination extends to seeing one of Santa's elves coming out of the forest- start worrying. This has gone past the imaginary friend stage… In all seriousness, though, stay positive and think of what you have to help you feel hopeful- <u>knowledge</u>, <u>skill</u>s, <u>equipment</u>, and a <u>plan</u>. Prepare. Don't lose hope. Empower yourself.

See you next month. Feel free to contact me with thoughts and stories. My only hope is that anything in one of these columns will be useful to someone. In the outdoors, as in life in general, a lot of things are never 100% sure. So we keep going to optimize, improve, make the best and feel good about ourselves and our efforts in the continual process. Please don't give up.

Outdoors Guy

Outdoors Guy It's All About Perspective

In survival, as in life, we feel better with a clear vision about our situation. It's a horrible feeling not knowing what to make of something and not knowing what to do or how to figure it out. This article is a mental exercise. It focuses on very basic considerations related to being in the wilderness. We have to start off presuming we're lost, stranded, and upset or bewildered.

The first reaction to an emergency may run a gamut of emotions- panic, regret, shock, grief, guilt, fear. Something has just happened, unplanned that's thrown you into an emotional state- a first reaction. It may have been an accident, a fire, collision, injury. Now what? There may have been someone seriously injured or someone may have perished. I hate talking in these terms, but surviving is sometimes a harsh brush with reality. Long story short- you have to be in your right mind. This is no time to let extreme emotions run away with you. Being emotional is your body's way of dealing with a shock. And it's OK! I may sound like I'm contradicting myself, but I'm not. You may need to cry, kick the tires, and compose yourself. This is normal, natural, and right. The point is, it can't last long. You have to do what it takes to get rid of feelings that will freeze you or cause you act irrationally.

Then get moving. People may be depending on you. At the very least, YOU are depending on you. A fair question to ask yourself would be, "Is this emotion (fear, anxiety, panic, regret, depression, helplessness) empowering me right now or disabling me right now?"

Assessment of the situation is the first step- realistically looking at the situation as it is NOW. (Regret will take you back uselessly. It doesn't matter now. NOW matters now.). Are there people injured? How can other people be directed to assist? Is someone in need of immediate first aid? If there are a number of people in need of assistance, who is priority depending on how severely hurt they are? Can someone be delegated the role of communicator and call 911? Is there possibility of something worse happening like fire spreading? Do people have to be removed from the immediate site to a safer spot?

Let's assume now that the immediate situation is under control. There is no life-threatening condition and no immediate danger from fire, gas, glass, wire, falling rocks, etc. You have the instinct that you may be here for a few days or longer. So now comes the next step...

Prioritize. You need protection from the elements. 7 basic factors come to mind- bugs, exposure to sunlight, heat, rain, winds, cold, and snow. Depending on the climate and time of year, priorities change. No worries about bugs and a sun burn in December. No worries about extreme cold in July, but insects and shade become important priorities. So calmly assess and prioritize. You need protection and what type of protection depends on conditions. Think, "Shade, protection from bugs, water, and perhaps rain." These will all be requirements that energies have to be directed towards.

Site selection is very important. Shelter has to be a high priority. You need to be near water. If you have a reasonable supply of water for the time being, go to the next item on the list- protection. Now that you have established a rational, sensible list of what your priorities are, the next step will be…

Taking stock of what you have in order to get the important tasks done. This includes checking into what the surrounding environment may have to offer. It sounds like so much of this is mental when you really need to be acting. I disagree. I believe that precious time and emotional resources are being saved by assessing the situation so you prioritize what needs to be done, and then again assessing what you need and what you can get to do the best job possible. Likely, someone will have to take the lead. And others will have to accept this arrangement or be adult enough to realize that they have to collaborate and not waste time arguing. Let's face it, "We're all it his together" is better than, "All in this at each-others' throats and accomplishing nothing useful or helpful."

For practicality's sake, think of what you need to be protected and comfortable. Are there long, strong branches you can use along with shorter ones to make a bed frame? Are there pine boughs available for bedding and helping wind proof a lean-to or A-Frame shelter? Are there dry leaves around useful as bedding but also as insulation from cold? In addition to what nature can provide, what have you got with you that can be improvised into something useful? If you have a tarp and rope you have a tent or ground sheet. If you have garbage bags you can create a makeshift mattress or leak-proof your shelter. A space blanket (better 2 space blankets) can help preserve precious body heat, keep out rain or provide shade. Are there any trees around with branches broken off at the right height and close enough together to allow you to begin fashioning a lean-to? Are there spare blankets in the vehicle? Is there a coffee can that you can use for boiling water or making into an improvised heater or stove Is there dry tinder, kindling, and fuel to be found nearby? Imagination is a gift here. Everything we humans ever devised was first imagined. You'll be proud of yourself when you see what you can come up with. Yes, you can.

Look at this situation the other way around. There's been an injury, an accident. People are sitting crying, full of grief and wishing they could wind the clock back 5 minutes or saying, "If only..." They become more anxiety ridden, panicky, and then depression sets in. They then just become still- almost like they've given up. (They <u>may</u> have indeed given up.) Or irrational behaviour has run wild. The battle is in the MIND. Nobody's saying this could've been avoided, or that it isn't serious. But it is what it is now and the only realistic thing to do is deal with it now. The mind is an amazing tool that needs to be focused. It can be- especially when it HAS to be. You're relying on it.

So, here's a re-cap. Calm down and put yourself into a state where you can think clearly. Assess the situation- both the immediate situation and with a view of addressing needs like shade, warmth, water, protection. Based on a realistic understanding of the situation, prioritize what tasks are most important, based on what elements you need protection from. Take stock of your resources, and then you can act in an empowered way, even if you tell yourself that you aren't helpless, that this situation can be made better. With a plan, you can always go back and work on doing things like making a shelter more secure, or working on signaling for help.

Several articles back I mentioned a person's mentality in relation to actually believing they CAN do this. Not giving up. This article is about HOW. Just to suggest a framework for your thoughts. Better decisions are made when you can accurately look at a situation. You'll actually be acting effectively sooner if you can do the thinking first.

Basic first aid demands being able to assess a situation and secure a scene. Isn't it funny how many things parallel survival situations? Life itself so often demands that we, to one degree or another, calm down and wait until we can think clearly and calmly again. And facing any challenge in life starts with having a perspective on the situation, and developing a Plan. Here's earnestly hoping nobody reading this has to face a serious crisis. I'm no expert on human psychology, but I do believe that we are much better off, more empowered, when we can see clearly what steps to take to gain control of a situation. Plus, a good assessment and a good plan provide much more hope and fuel for being positive. As a final thought, keep busy. It is far better to be occupied with a meaningful, productive task than stuck and inactive. If you're seeing positive results from your actions and you feel you're on the right track, good! This wasn't meant to preach or be a psychology lesson. Just some suggestions that hopefully could provide a more useful perspective on a situation where you're being challenged so you better rise to meet that challenge.

Have Faith. Maintain Hope.

Till next time,

Outdoors Guy

Outdoors Guy- Survival Kit

Last month's article talked about the intangible: Mental and emotional factors in surviving. I don't want to be abstract very often. So this month, and in the following months, it's going to be practical. Everybody has their own personal "Top 10" items they'd stow in a survival pack. So here it goes- my choices. Actually, not 10- it'll be stretched into what I could pack efficiently into 1 backpack. Some items are non-negotiable- in any situation- your true "Top 10" items. This is my favourite article because I got to play with all my "junk"- any excuse to take it out and look at it and feel proud and dream of my next trip…What's more- I really had to think about it- all the necessities in one backpack. It's a constant debate- and it's FUN!!

Let's begin with some common sense. Traveling up North in winter weather… you <u>have</u> an emergency kit in addition to a survival kit. Flares, emergency candles, extra water, booster cables, a shovel, power bars, maps, tread racks for when you get stuck in the snow, gas tank topped up as well as de-icer fluid, cell phone charged, some hand and foot warmers. This is just common sense. These are items that involve much less hassle to pack than will be involved if you got stuck and you <u>didn't</u> pack them.

So you are the prepared type of person. Good for you! Let's now to get down to some further basics... First, consider where you're venturing to. Does anyone else know your route? Is your destination isolated? How long do you intend to stay? Have you several means of communication IF you encounter an emergency? Have you checked the weather reports and road conditions? I know it seems like I'm taking a long time getting on with the focus I started with but it doesn't start when you're on the road or on the trail- <u>it starts at home with your planning</u>. The trip you are planning demands preparation- so will the trip you <u>aren't</u> planning on. Consider what the <u>essentials</u> are to surviving- Shelter/Warmth/Protection from the elements, Water (uncontaminated) in a steady supply, Location and Communication (knowing where you are and being able to use a few basic skills with a compass, map, GPS System, Personal Locator Beacon), Food, Safety and First Aid, Fire. Your list of critical items going into a survival kit MUST allow you to address these needs.

What follows is my opinion but a lot of people will agree that certain things are indispensable. Here's my "Top 40". NOTE: Some items can't be carried on a backpack- so we'll proceed with the understanding that we'll get as much in as little space as possible- deal?

1. A good quality bush knife. Defense, building, hunting.
2. Rope- 550 lb. test- at least 50-100 ft.
3. Space blanket. Packs up into a tiny space. Can save you from freezing, serve as an emergency tarp for a temporary shelter, even signal to planes. Beware- these aren't aluminum foil so don't bring one near a flame. There are even

solar blanket emergency tents available which pack into a very small space.

4. Good quality Swiss Army Knife or Multi-tool. My favourite straps around my belt and contains a hammer, mini-saw, screwdriver blades, knife blade, pliers, bottle opener and can opener. A gift I'll always treasure from one of my former students, it's a top-line multi-tool with all kinds of applications.

5. A tarp (at <u>least</u> 8' by 10') to build an emergency shelter or serve as a ground sheet. The larger the better if using it as your main shelter.

6. A hexamine stove with hexamine fuel tablets. You can buy extra fuel cells. This device fits into your pocket.

7. Lighters- butane at least a 5-pack. Torch lighters are best- very wind resistant.

8. Self-powered flashlight. Mine has a handle with drill bits. Very handy!

9. First Aid Kit- **<u>Spend the money and get a top quality one</u>** with triangular bandages, antiseptics, scissors, sting stop, etc. Learn how to use the items it contains by taking a registered First Aid course. *Carried separately. This HAS to rank high in essential gear. *Include any medications such as anti-histamines, painkillers, prescription drugs, etc. *Vitamin pills are essential because your diet may depend on what you can locate, trap, etc. (Carried separately)

10. Cell phone with car charger.
    Water Skin)- FULL.

11. Emergency Rain Poncho. Again, you can buy these at outdoor stores in packets that fold down into very small spaces.
12. Mosquito netting- at <u>least</u> hood and vest. (Your bug repellant may run out- then what?)
13. Metal cup. Seem strange? You can use it for preparing a hot drink, purifying water by boiling it.
14. Mess kit. Small pots, plates, knife, fork, spoon. Fry-pan with a folding handle. *You CAN make do with a small pan and the metal cup.
15. Folding Camp Saw.
16. Hatchet.
17. Personal hygiene kit- soap, toothpaste and toothbrush, facecloth, small towel, etc. (Carried in a small kit).
18. Compass/maps.
19. Whistle. Mine comes with whistle, compass and thermometer all in one.
20. Mirror for signalling.
21. Magnifying glass- secondary source of fire and useful for removing splinters/locating stingers.
22. Orange garbage bags (I know- here he goes with his garbage bags again...) Emergency rain ponchos, rain tarps, groundsheets, signaling devices, pillows and bedding mattresses (filled with leaves), rain catchers, solar still and transpiration bags, storage for clothes and bedding to keep dry.
23. Garden trowel. Use for digging a fire pit, latrine.

24. Mini-fishing kit containing a few hooks, sinkers, line, float, and some lures. (*More about this in an upcoming issue.) Fishing line can be used as rope in shelter construction.
25. Tent pegs- metal.
26. Duct tape.
27. Baking Soda. A must for yellow-jacket stings. Store in First Aid Kit.
28. Sunblock & Hat. <u>Sunglasses</u>. Even in winter. Glare can cause snow blindness.
29. Insect repellant.
30. Anti-Itch Cream. Costs About $8 to $10 a tube- but it's a bargain. Believe me.
31. Toilet paper. Can insulate a jacket along with dry leaves. Try not to depend on it to start fires- you'll rue the fact that you ran out of it! Rather- use the inner roll to create a fire bundle of dry tinder or bring a few rolls loosely filled with dryer lint to kindle a fire.
32. Metal coat hanger. *Please refer back to Issue #1. It has a lot of uses. Or as small grill rack.
33. Snare wire.
34. Emergency Candles. Compact and can burn for a long time.
35. Waterproof matches. The benefits of a fire can't be over-stated. Have at least 3 or 4 options available.
36. Coffee filters to improvise a water purification device. See my Issue #2 for details using sand, charcoal, coffee filters and a pop bottle to filter water. Remember to boil or add

chlorine or water purification tablets to kill bacteria. Or, just pack water purification tablets.

37. Drink packets and power bars.
38. Sewing Kit.
39. Pocket hand warmers- 6-10
40. Red or orange surveyor's tape- marking trails.

OK, so there's a list. Got it down to 40! Please remember: The idea isn't about a numerical limit, it's about what will fit that you'll need. It is to explore the possibility of getting the most effective equipment for the least space and weight. It was fun, and a challenge, packing my own survival backpack to see what I could fit without too much weight and still zip it up. Remember the essentials of survival- Warmth/Shelter/Protection, Communication, Water, Safety, Food, Fire. Remember to keep personal ID, photos, $ in a waterproof bag. You select and pack gear based on the essentials needed for survival. The idea is always to give yourself as many decent trump cards to play as you can- but also to give yourself as much versatility as you can. Items such as a multi-tool, knife, space blanket, tarp, rope have multiple uses and give you a lot of elbow room for improvisation. In a future article, I want to tie these ideas together for something like a hiking trip.

Challenge yourself to work on your own complete survival kit. Think seriously of what can fit and also what you can carry on you or with you that won't take up extra space. EXTRA NOTE: *1 more essential item is a sturdy walking stick. Use it to avoid falls, clear brush from your face, defense, as a ridgepole for a shelter, navigate around swamps. Slightly taller than your own height, your hand fits around it, strong/supple. It has multiple uses.

Here's some "homework" for you. Take my list and beside each item write the need that the item addresses. Example: Tarp-shelter/collecting water. The more you can see multiple uses for any 1 item the better. You're using your creativity and problem solving skills.

I personally have a lot of fun arguing with myself (I'm the only one that listens) about what goes in the Top 10-25 items. I constantly re-arrange the list. Have fun trying it yourself. Remember that the Top items are the really NON-NEGOTIABLES! Rope, bush knife, space blanket, flashlight, multi-tool, tarp, lighters, etc. There's always that trade-off between weight and space balanced by absolute necessity. By all means feel free to e-mail me with your own list of "must-have" items. Stay safe, be prepared. Practice packing as much stuff into as little space as you can. Handy skill if you have a small car!

Always Plan Ahead and Keep Safe.

Outdoors Guy- The Humble Garbage Bag

In this issue we'll discuss garbage bags and shopping bags. How can they be used in a survival situation? We'll start with a garbage bag. Before you set out on an outdoor adventure pack 2 or 3 <u>orange</u> good quality garbage bags in your survival kit (more about this in a future issue). Here is the reason for orange. In a survival situation, orange contrasts with practically <u>everything</u> else in your environment- similar to why hunters wear orange while out on a trail. With an orange garbage bag you can easily make a flag with a branch to signal passing planes/helicopters and alert them to your presence. Green and black garbage bags are much harder to spot. *It should also be noted that, in addition to the orange garbage bag, you should always carry a highly reflective piece (like a mirror- they're commercially sold) and a sound alert such as a Fox-40™ whistle. (There is a make available that combines thermometer, compass, and whistle along with fancier ones with even more).

Use #2: The lowly garbage bag can be almost immediately converted to a rain jacket. Now have some common sense and <u>do</u> cut a hole in the front <u>just under the seam</u> (where the bottom of the garbage bag would be in normal use) so you can breathe and even have a sort of visor to keep rain off your face. Cut holes in the sides if you wish so you can use your arms.

Use #3: You can use the garbage bag (particularly if you cut it open to maximum size) as a rain tarp, ground tarp, or even crude tent. As a rain tarp it can be draped over a rope or over a branch frame. Get creative! As a ground tarp it helps keep you drier and put a layer between the cold, damp, and bugs. You'd need several to make a rudimentary tent and the sides have to be weighted down onto the ground with stones or long branches. Obviously, you can't peg the sides down like you could with a real tarp since you'd just rip your material. The easiest may be to drape the garbage bags over a small rope tied between 2 trees, like a traditional "A" frame tent. Your life can be made a whole lot more comfortable by sleeping on some bedding. Dry leaves smell nice, have to be piled high (at least 5 times more than you'd think because they flatten out while you're sleeping on them), and they hold heat amazingly well. You can even use them to burrow down into for night or 2 in the fall (unless it's going to rain!)

Use #4: Water: Laying the garbage bag out with the 4 corners raised can catch a lot of rain. You can create a "solar still" by digging a 2 ft. hole, piling the bottom with green foliage (be careful-don't use poisonous plants!), placing a cup in the middle of the bottom of the hole to catch condensed water, covering the hole with the garbage bag and weighting it down over the hole with a small stone placed in the middle of the top of the garbage bag so that condensed water will drip into the cup underneath. The sun will cause water from the foliage to condense onto the bottom of the garbage bag and then it falls into the cup. It is distilled already. *Note: in a real emergency you may need to build several of these if there's no other water source available.

Garbage bags can also be tied onto the ends of branches with plenty of leaves to catch water. This is known as the "Transpiration" Method.

Use #5: Referring back to the tent mentioned above...you want to get a good night's sleep but you forgot your pillow. Simply stuff the normal sized shopping bag full of DRY leaves from a non-poisonous tree (maple, oak... very "fluffy" if I do say) and then tie off the open end like you would a garbage bag. Put the "pillow" inside a T-shirt (you don't want to sleep with your face buried in plastic) and you have a pillow. Use willow leaves and it's a willow pillow. (Who knows, maybe the idea will market someday. LOL)

A life-saving use for the garbage bag is to use it to collect rain water if you're running short of clean water for drinking. Simply lay the sheet down and elevate the four corners so as to form a "bowl". This water doesn't have to be boiled. If you really anticipate needing as much water as possible for an extended period of time, put out as many rain catchers as possible. In a pinch, they can also be used to store your water. Keep the bag safe from punctures.

*Related Tip: With regard to those leaves...remember you can use a bundle of twigs and branches tied together to rake up dry leaves far faster than you could bare-handed. (Art of Improv I)

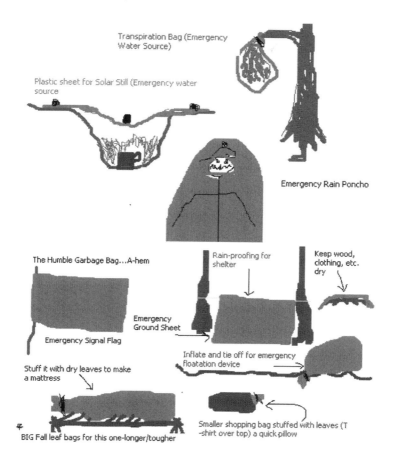

Transpiration Bag (Emergency Water Source)

Plastic sheet for Solar Still (Emergency water source

Emergency Rain Poncho

The Humble Garbage Bag...A-hem

Rain-proofing for shelter

Keep wood, clothing, etc. dry

Emergency Ground Sheet

Emergency Signal Flag

Inflate and tie off for emergency floatation device

Stuff it with dry leaves to make a mattress

BIG Fall leaf bags for this one-longer/tougher

Smaller shopping bag stuffed with leaves (T-shirt over top) a quick pillow

Navigating by the Sun, Moon, and Stars

This article is meant to "give people direction". You know how we're all looking for direction in life? I took this literally. Let's say you are lost and are without a GPS or compass. You know the approximate location of say, the road you want to get back to or where your campsite is. Since this deals with relative location, (where you are in relation to where you want to go) here's some tips.

If you have an analog watch (remember those watches with the big hand and the little hand...). Point the hour hand directly at the sun. Now bisect the angle formed by the hour hand and 12 o'clock. This line points you directly to the South. Using the line pointing South and extending it backwards will point you North. I am very used to looking at maps which are oriented towards the North with West on my left and East on my right. Simply reverse these directions since the line you formed by angle bisection points to the South. So, West will be on your right hand side and East will be on your left hand side. Now you have established the 4 basic directions. Here's another cool thing about an analog watch. Since it is divided into 12 hours, every hour equals 30°, as on a compass. So you can fine tune your directions. Start with North at 0°. South is 180°, or 6 o'clock.

Now for the moon- if the moon is new or nearly new, try this. Follow the moon's "chin". It will point you approximately South. If the moon is waning it will be on your other side. Do the same thing. Follow the moon's "chin" again. It is pointing South. One further interesting fact: If the moon rises before dark, the lit side is facing west. If the moon rises after dark, the bright side is facing east.

Now to turn to the stars- you'll feel the wonder of ancient peoples gazing upwards. The North Star, Polaris, maintains a fixed position in the sky. Locate the Big Dipper and find the last 2 stars on the end of the ladle. Mentally draw a line from the bottom of the ladle to the top and extend the distance of the line roughly 4 to 5 times. This line will point to the North Star, and you will be looking North. To clarify: these are the 2 stars farthest from the handle. Once you've found the North Star and are looking North, then you can again mark the other 3 directions by thinking that behind you is South, West is on your left, and East is on your right.

I've included diagrams to illustrate these ideas and make them clearer. You're doing what mariners from ages long past have done before today's sophisticated equipment came along. Hopefully, you'll be equipped with a GPS or compass and map. But if you're stuck, these ideas may help.

Just another couple of quick thoughts... If you are venturing out into an unfamiliar terrain, mark your trail with orange surveyor's tape. Think about the "For Dummies" series of books. Make your trail markings easy enough for ANYONE to follow. This can help (even save your life) in 2 ways. 1. You can backtrack and find your own way out. 2. If you are injured, giving your point of entry by cell phone (you DID remember to leave a trip plan with 2 responsible people, didn't you?) will provide searchers with a starting point to track you. The surveyor's tape should lead them right to your location. By the way, you DID bring a fully charged cell phone, right?

Finally, it may be very helpful to use a landmark to get you back to where you where you want to go. Note any large landmarks, church steeples, large rocks, the lakeshore, a building, etc. Even write them down as you travel further so you can use them as reference points on the way back. You can now use your watch compass to plot the direction towards the landmarks. If you veer off course, try to correct course as quickly as possible.

I'd like to end by offering this tip for telling time remaining with the Sun. It's getting on evenin' and you reckon you should be heading home. The sun is sinking. Hold your hand out at full length toward the sun. Multiply the number of fingers between the sun and the horizon times 15- in other words, roughly 15 minutes per finger between the sun and horizon.

Next month's article is meant to compliment this one-Signaling. Use all your senses, but most importantly common sense. Be aware, be prepared, be safe. Our high tech. devices are the best and fastest way to navigate and communicate with. CARRY THEM. USE THEM.

Outdoors Guy

<u>Orienting Towards the South Using an Analog Watch</u>

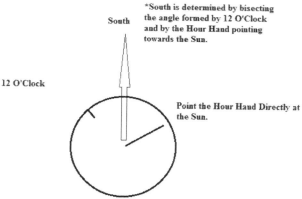

South

12 O'Clock

*South is determined by bisecting the angle formed by 12 O'Clock and by the Hour Hand pointing towards the Sun.

Point the Hour Hand Directly at the Sun.

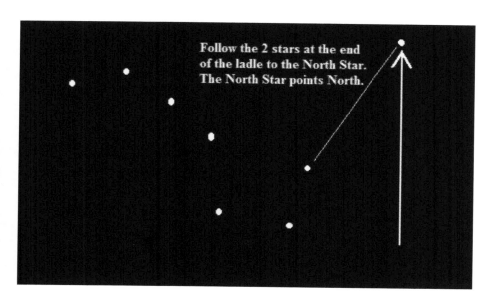

Follow the 2 stars at the end of the ladle to the North Star. The North Star points North.

Follow the Moon's "chin". A line from the top tip of the crescent to the bottom tip points you roughly South. Note: A Waxing Moon is moving from East to South. A Waning Moon is moving from South to West.

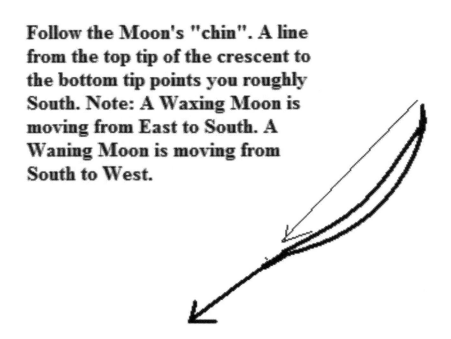

Getting Your Signals Straight

Now for the companion article to Navigation- namely signaling. There are technological tools that are amazing available to let you know where you are and let others know where you are- PLB (Personal Locator Beacon), SPOT, GPS Systems, and, yes, the cell phone. These devices make it easier for Search and Rescue Personnel to find you, so, as I said in my last article: "Buy them, carry them, USE them." Spend time learning how they work and what they are designed to do.

Just to stay on this track for a few moments, you can make finding you a whole lot easier just in case you are injured and need assistance. You may also lose track of your whereabouts. Again: Did you leave a Trip Plan with at least 2 responsible people before you left? Is your cell phone fully charged? Do you have a primary system of location: a map and compass, GPS System? Have you packed vital equipment such as water and First Aid Supplies? Do you carry flares, battery cables, candles, water, power bars, etc. to go on trips?

Ok. I know this sounds ridiculous for a trip to the corner store. But you've probably figured out that this article isn't really intended for the aficionado of the corner store. So here's the focus.

1. Be PREPARED. You can make it so much easier for yourself and others if you carry the right equipment, make the proper arrangements, and anticipate having a Plan B. Even in an accident you stand better odds by having tools available so that the situation isn't made worse by having fewer options. Give yourself something to work with.

2. Let's assume it's back to basics and your cell phone is missing or out of power. You don't have a locating device with you and you have to get someone's attention because you're lost, become ill, injured. Here are some cards you CAN still play. I recognize that bad things can happen to even the most prepared people. Please excuse me if anything in my tone in this or the previous article sounds belittling of someone who may have just forgotten an important piece of equipment. (Suggestion: Have a checklist

before you leave- ensure everything you need is with you AND that it's working properly). With all that, things can still "happen". So...

Think in terms of human senses. The more options you have to reach people by any means the better your chances. So, being a former teacher, I turn to what we talked about in student learning styles: Visual and Auditory. We'll be adding Olfactory to the whole strategy.

Begin with the time of day. You'll do better if you can start during the daylight hours. If you're in remote camping or survival mode, you may have built a shelter that is well sealed against sunlight, bugs, cold winds, and rain, but is out of sight. A well-constructed shelter will often be naturally camouflaged. So you need an open area from which to signal.

Here are some ways to use sight to alert people as to your location.

1. A signal mirror. Inexpensive at most outdoor shops. A very good improvisation can be made with just a CD. It has the added benefit of having a sighting hole thru the middle so that, if a plane is passing, you can look thru the hole and thus aim your visual signal towards it more accurately. Use a pie pan, beer can- anything shiny.
2. You knew this was coming. An orange garbage bag tied to a stick makes a flag. With the exception of leaves in the fall, there is nothing else around to compete with the colour orange. Searchers will be looking for, among other things, colours that contrast with the environment that make you

stand out. Even a large red bandana can serve to create a makeshift flag. Be resourceful. If you have a brightly coloured tent, move it into the open. *Exception: NOT if lightning is a possibility.

3. Fire. A signal fire should be set up in a clearing. Burn damp wood to create denser smoke. In a real emergency situation, people have burned tires of their vehicles because the smoke is black and very dense. Motor oil will do the same thing, especially dirty motor oil. Be careful to stand upwind. The fumes are toxic.

4. See if you can roll a couple of logs or large rocks together to form a large "V" in a clearly visible spot. This is a universal signal for help. Try to find a clearing with enough area for a helicopter to land if you are in a very remote area.

5. As was mentioned in the previous article, marking a trail with surveyor's tape, which is bright orange, can both direct you back to your point of entry into the woods, or direct a rescue team right to your present location if you've been hiking and are lost/stranded.

Now Listen Up...

1. Carry a whistle. There are commercial whistles available that also have compasses and even thermometers built into one unit. These are usually shrill and carry a long way. Especially if you think you may hear a search group approaching. From what I've read, bears will usually do their best to avoid human contact. So if you think your signal may be heard, don't hesitate- use it.

2. Pots and pans. Nobody like it when the kids are playing drums on pots and pans or the neighbour's teens are jamming in the basement. So here's a clue. The sound is LOUD and very difficult not to notice. It's not the usual sound one hears in the wild. So this makes for a sound that can be heard and followed. If you rescue crew are metal fans, they'll gravitate towards it naturally.

Finally...If You Can Smell 'Em, You Can Tell 'Em."

If there is a wind then the smell from a fire will carry for a certain distance- if it's a very smoky fire, (white or black), it can lead searchers right to you. This is not to imply that you avoid taking a bath for 6 months prior to the trip. What if people are more than a mile away from your location?

It would be funny if you had some kind of outrageous sign in your possession. Why not even carry a colourful flag? It is rare to see a For Sale sign or a Star Spangled Banner in the middle of a clearing surrounded by dense brush. People won't be thinking... Hmmmm... American bears?" Get creative! Who's going to laugh at your hot pink Bermuda shorts? What's most important here? Think about what you can use and/or set up that looks out of place <u>that draws attention because it contrasts with its surroundings</u>.

As always the same note sounds. Be prepared. Have the right equipment. Leave a detailed plan behind with at least 2 responsible people. Anticipate, but don't be paranoid of, things that could go wrong. Provide yourself with as many options as you can. Have a Plan B. Know how to use that First Aid Kit. Use technical equipment. It's far faster and more efficient. Why do things the hard way when it can be made so much easier? And lastly, remember that there are still a few tricks up your sleeve if the worst happens. Don't give up hope. If you even remembered to leave a plan with someone and an estimated time of return, they'll begin to get concerned if you haven't shown up after a reasonable length of time.

FINAL TIP: Don't make the mistake of planning to return home at dusk or after dark if you're hiking- particularly if you're alone. This can be a FATAL mistake. Plan to return with plenty of daylight left. That way you have time if you need to set up emergency signals when people can best spot them. Searchers also have time to track you while it's still light out- thereby greatly increasing your chances of an early rescue. Your most important sense is common sense. Please, as always, have fun and be safe. Your Pal,

Outdoors Guy

Introduction to Shelters

It can be said that there are 2 types of shelters- the one you carry with you that you've brought everything for (you have a tent in the back of the SUV), and the one you HAVE to make because you're stuck in a remote place. We can take it from here. Now there's 2 types again-short-term (to get you thru a few nights warm, dry and safe), and long term (thinking that you may have to survive here for a while).

I said in a previous article that planning is everything. It IS!! Do you have spare candles, water, matches, a tarp (or better, 2), power bars, rope, a knife, flashlight, rain and or cold weather clothing, batteries, lighters, digging tool, multi-tool, camp saw, emergency (solar) blanket, sleeping bags/blankets, cooking utensils,...?

OK. I hear you saying, "All this to go to the grocery store?" No. The thinking is that the further you're travelling and the more remote the area, the more you should plan on. Your surroundings may furnish you with some necessary materials. But you can't depend on that- or take it for granted.

Let's say we're travelling to a more remote area in the north country in the Spring/Summer... heat, rain, bugs to deal with.

Autumn- a nice time of year- no bugs (or few bugs), beautiful colours, rain and sudden changes of temperature. Leaves are available for sheltering and bedding. Winter- OK…no bugs but it's cold and the snow's deep. We have to anticipate based on season and surroundings.

What I'd like to begin discussing is shelter. If you bring materials with you, you won't have to find them. Let's assume, however that we first need a suitable location- one that offers some protection from the wind and rain. Some shade and is safe from natural threats like falling branches, flooding, avalanches. And it should at least offer a suitable, large enough, space to build a camp. We have to be near enough to a source of water. We have to have some clear open space to signal. (Did you remember the orange garbage bags????? Good for you!) And, bonus points… a site which may have natural materials around.

This article will open the discussion with natural shelters and short-term sheltering ideas. PLEASE remember- the more materials you have brought with you, the more you'll have to work with and hence the less time you'll have to waste looking around and thinking about how to improvise.

A sheltered area under the boughs of a larger pine or spruce tree may afford space. We'll have to watch broken braches with sharp edges. There has to be enough clearance to crawl and hopefully sit. A drawback may be that it`ll be hard to enclose enough to keep all bugs out so the mosquito net and repellent better be packed. Stacking more boughs or even wrapping a larger tarp around the trunk over some lower branches can do the trick. Be careful of a flame in here! The lower branches may be dried out and they are LOADED with turpentine. But you can potentially make a shelter to serve that will keep out some of the elements.

I have slept in a huge pile of leaves when I was certain the weather would remain dry that night. It's comfortable, and warm, and the leaves smell nice too. I just had to re-fluff my "mattress" a few times because leaves compress down to a thin hard surface. The trick is to pile up PLENTY to start with. As mentioned in a previous article, bring some large, sturdy garbage bags with you and stuff the leaves in them for a mattress. Use a smaller one for a pillow- with a T-shirt over top so your head isn't buried in plastic.

The tarp can really come into its own now, especially if you've got guy-ropes pre-tied and tent stakes on hand. Below are 2 possible configurations you might wish to consider- even experiment with in your own backyard so it becomes second-nature once you're in the outdoors.

The back end of this can be easily dropped to offer more shelter from rain and prevent the tent from becoming a wind tunnel. It also shuts out bugs from one side. A larger tarp is better. At least you won't feel as cramped and you'll have room to store your stuff. A smaller tarp is then ideal as a ground sheet. Move your makeshift mattress in and lay your blanket/sleeping bag over top. Having mosquito screening for the "front door" isn't a bad idea- or use a tent rain tarp and peg it closed with something like clothes pegs. Bring a flashlight inside with you. You'll have to leave some venting space for fresh air if you don't have mosquito netting, so probably better to have some. *Alternately...why not use some porch screen you just "happen to have brought with you"? Fresh air, you can always drape a rain tarp across the front if it gets wet, and you can thumb your nose at the bugs. A blanket draped may be another consideration.

Finally, in a lower-lying area where water may pool, you may wish to dig a run-off trench around the perimeter of your shelter. Lighting a fire (not TOO close) can help with warmth and smoke from punky wood will help drive bugs away- You just don't want the smoke blowing into your shelter, so why not close the front and then just climb in when you're ready to bed down? Check for mosquitoes before laying down. This can save you some real aggravation. Have a walking stick/knife/bat/golf club handy for protection and sleep tight. Soon- more of what you can do with a tarp. From there we'll progress to wood shelters.

Stay Sheltered! It May Not Be Much, But It's Home!

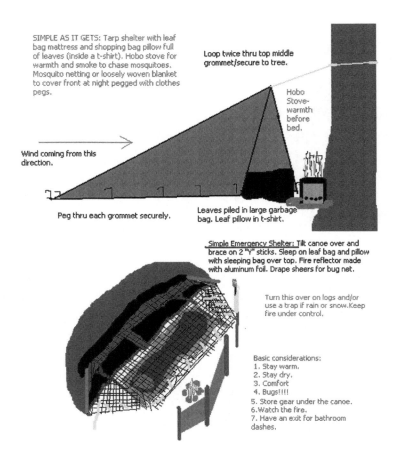

SIMPLE AS IT GETS: Tarp shelter with leaf bag mattress and shopping bag pillow full of leaves (inside a t-shirt). Hobo stove for warmth and smoke to chase mosquitoes. Mosquito netting or loosely woven blanket to cover front at night pegged with clothes pegs.

Loop twice thru top middle grommet/secure to tree.

Hobo Stove- warmth before bed.

Wind coming from this direction.

Peg thru each grommet securely.

Leaves piled in large garbage bag. Leaf pillow in t-shirt.

Simple Emergency Shelter: Tilt canoe over and brace on 2 "Y" sticks. Sleep on leaf bag and pillow with sleeping bag over top. Fire reflector made with aluminum foil. Drape sheers for bug net.

Turn this over on logs and/or use a trap if rain or snow.Keep fire under control.

Basic considerations:
1. Stay warm.
2. Stay dry.
3. Comfort
4. Bugs!!!!
5. Store gear under the canoe.
6.Watch the fire.
7. Have an exit for bathroom dashes.

What You Can Do With a Tarp

A tarp is one of the most useful and versatile pieces of equipment you can carry. I'm going to start with a basic shape- an upside-down "V", and take it from there. Let's begin with some earthy humour…You can make 2 identical tarp shelters, place a CD player between them…and have a "stereo-tarp". (Now you can appreci-ate why I chose education over stand-up comedy as a career.)

To make a simple tent you can choose 1 of 2 options. The first involves obtaining 4 sturdy branches about an inch in diameter-one pair for the front and the other pair for the back. Lash them together at the top leaving about 2 or 3 inches. Next, take some rope, make a loop at one end and peg it into the ground. Run the rope to the front "A" and wind it around your lashing knot and then extend it out to the back "A". The length between the 2 "A" 's depends on how long your tarp is. The depth of the tent depends on how much tarp you have. Wind the rope around the top of the back "A", then pull it SECURELY to make the frame stand up. Make another loop and peg this down at the back. If done properly, this frame will hold very well. I've tried it in brisk wind..

A simple option involves simply tying your rope between 2 trees securely. Make sure you don't open up a tunnel for the wind by opening your tent right into it. I made this mistake…ONCE…

In the case of winds and rain, you can simply drop the end facing the wind to the ground. This will give you more protection. This is called a "Quick Shelter".

Tip: If it's really hot out, rig up another tarp 6 inches above your shelter tarp. This provides shade. You can also give yourself some breeze by raising the guy line holding the ridge of the tarp a foot so that air can circulate. Use the grommets on the sides of the tarp This way you still have shade and you have air moving as well. Drop the tarp tent back down at night.

If you have a hammock, you can use the tarp again to provide shade. Just string the ridgeline high enough to hang the tarp. This works best if you can anchor the tarp down to the ground with rope and pegs at least at all four corners.

Remember that a tarp can also be a groundsheet to help keep you dry and pile leaves or pine/spruce boughs on for bedding.

We can now think of how to vary the configuration of the trap. Instead of a triangular prism, visualize a rectangular prism. If you string a guy line between 2 trees you can fold the tarp to provide a roof, back wall, and a groundsheet. You now have 3 of the 6 faces of the rectangular prism for shelter. This can really be a better set-up if the open face of your tarp shelter is facing your fire pit. You can make this even more heat efficient by building a fire reflector (*See diagram) on the other side of the tarp. Covering the 2 sides of the shelter will require another tarp or sheet of some kind. Ideally (I'm thinking) 2 6 x 6ft. tarps will work. You can tie the pieces together at the grommet holes. As another option, a space blanket, 2 garbage bags, and some mosquito netting (old drape sheers) can hang over the front. Now you have a fairly secure shelter, enclosed on 5 sides, with netting to keep out the bugs. It obviously takes some work to piece together, but it keeps the weather out. (*Again, please see the diagrams for some suggested set-ups.)

A good rule of thumb is to set the shelter up with respect to the size of your bed. Allow yourself time to set you bedroll/sleeping bag up with a mat or bedding made from soft, dry leaves/boughs. Better to crawl into something ready-made when the sun goes down and the vampirish predators appear. Remember to watch your fire. Sparks can fly (no pun intended)! The heat reflector will help smoke rise straight up but the wind can always shift. It is important to have the back section of the tarp facing the oncoming wind. This has 2 advantages:

1. You are sheltered from the wind.
2. The wind is blowing smoke AWAY from you, not AT you.

Here's a really creative use for a tarp. Lay the tarp down and cover with dry leaves. Now lay down and roll the tarp around yourself! A sleeping bag! Never mind about getting leaves all over yourself. When you were a kid, it was a riot.

A clean tarp can be spread out to collect water in an emergency.

I must emphasize, keep the tarp clean and dry. Carry 2 or 3 with at least 1 LARGE tarp.

A final thought would be to build yourself a tipi. I prefer setting up 4 uprights instead of 3 for a simple mathematical reason. 4 uprights create a square floor, which has double the area of a triangle. You need a large tarp for this- Likely 2 large tarps. The space you get inside is worth it! You can even stand up if the tipi is large enough. If it starts to ran, just drape a garbage bag around the top and tie down. You have some space to store your gear. Now get some sleep.

The tarp is a versatile tool that can be used as far as your imagination can take you. The diagrams are just some suggestions. It's always fun to try your own design. Basics: A good shelter keeps out rain and winds. It is stable and secure. One of my "Tricks" in making a tarp stretch tight is to wind my rope around a grommet hole and then pull it.

Hope this information is helpful both as a camping tool and a survival tool. If you forget a tent, or it rips, you have your tarps. Keep an roll of duct tape handy for repairs. You can also buy grommet replacement kits.

Tight Lines- Safe and Comfy,

Your Pal,

Outdoors Guy

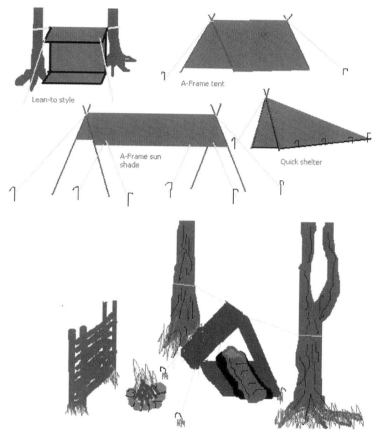

Lean-to style

A-Frame tent

A-Frame sun shade

Quick shelter

Simple Tarp Tent: DON'T construct it so the wind blows thru OR in the direction of the wind. In a pinch, you can drop the back end in the direction of wind/rain/snow to add heat retention and help keep dry.

Guyline has to be TIGHT. tent stakes/pegs have to pointed at a 45 degree angle AWAY from the tent and DEEP into the ground. If your tarp doesn't have grommets (it should) use rocks/logs/sand bags made from shopping bags. Entrance can face a small fire (damp wood helps keep mosquitoes away). Cover front entrance with tent tarp.

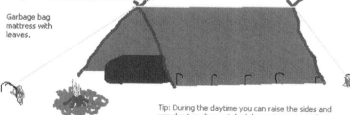

Garbage bag mattress with leaves.

Of course-fire not to close-put out at bed. time.

Tip: During the daytime you can raise the sides and use short guylines- staked down. An airy sun shade.

209

Outdoors Guy- Wood Shelters- Lean-to's and A-Frames.

Four basic designs come to mind when discussing wood shelters: the tipi, the lean-to, and the A-Frame shelter. A cabin is something I haven't attempted yet- but it's on my list. The tipi has been discussed in relation to tarps. We'll be talking about the Lean-to and A-Frame in this issue.

Lean-to's are the simplest wood shelters to build, requiring the least amount of time, energy and materials. Simply find two trees that are reasonably close together and use a long branch as a <u>ridgepole</u>. This is the basic "cornerstone", if you will. Now begin lining the ridgepole with sturdy branches placed horizontally from the ridgepole to the ground. You'll have to consider several factors. First of all, which direction do the prevailing winds come from? Often (and I don't know why) the prevailing winds at my favourite campsite are southwest. This is important for two reasons. 1. You need protection from the sun during the day in hot summer weather as well as colder winds in the evening and at night. The lean-to is an open air shelter so heat cannot be trapped inside as it could be with an enclosed shelter. Add to this the ever-present possibility of rain. If it comes at you while you're facing it, the lean-to will offer no protection. 2. Smoke from your fire can be blown right back at you if the wind shifts.

Not to make this too dismal, there are options and ways you can maximize your protection with a lean-to. Here are some suggestions:

-use LONG branches and slant them more than 50° so that rain/snow will slide off rather than collect- the steeper the slant and the longer the branches the better.

-To increase protection and insulation from the wind, line your uprights with pine branches, as thickly as possible. The broken branch end should be pointed upright. Over this layer, add a tarp, several garbage bags, large sheets of dead birch bark, or even a solar blanket. If it isn't going to rain at night, layer the wall thickly- then use the space blanket for warmth. This is your first line of defense against cold. Better wrapped around your body where it can do its primary job- to retain body heat.

-You can use a tarp to enclose the front of the lean-to if you have a large enough one available.

-The sides of a lean to can be enclosed in exactly the same way the wall is enclosed. Simply cut branches down to size as you lean them against an upright. (*See diagram) Now you have protection from 3 sides. Remember: The steeper the lean-to, the more it sheds rain. The deeper the lean-to, the more space you create for yourself. You DO create more space with branches that are laid down with a gradual slope, but you have to consider rain as a factor. It must also be pointed out that you don't only have to use ONE layer of branches for your overlay. Why not make a better seal against weather by overlaying 2 or 3 layers of branches? (Make SURE the ridgepole is STRONG and SECURELY ANCHORED!)

-Now you have your luxury semi-condo constructed. How about some comfort? There are several options when it comes to a bed. This will largely be limited by the space available inside the lean-to. The simplest materials (that also smell the best and insulate the best) are pine/spruce boughs and DRY leaves. These should be layered as thickly as possible. Leaves compress quickly and then you'd think you were on the ground again. Spruce branches keep the air fresh smelling, and are a soft bed. Given a choice, I'd go leaves (thick!), spruce or pine boughs, and then another, thinner layer of leaves. Check for branches that'll stick into you before you lay down and have to remove them.

A step up is to build a platform bed by laying slats (smooth and straight) along 2 long logs. Alternately, you can make 4 tripods out of inch thick 12-16 inch branches, lay 2 sturdy long branches to form the sides of the bed, then lay down as many cross pieces as you need to. You have to be comfortable. That means plenty of crosspieces so you a) distribute your weight, and b) so that part of your body isn't falling into a space with no support. Then overlay again with leaves and boughs.

-Finally, build a fire reflector. This will help radiate heat back towards you and also helps with smoke since the wall of the fire reflector tends to make smoke rise. Having it blow in your face is nasty! The fire reflector is built by using 2 slanted uprights supported by two "Y" sticks. You then stack branches as closely as possible up to height of 3 feet. This gives more protection from the wind, prevents the wind from blowing smoke and sparks at you, and creates vital re-radiation of warmth. Watch that fire! Low and steady. The insurance agent will be furious if you burn down your brand new dream home the first night.

-Finally, why not try adding some drape sheers as mosquito netting over the front face of the lean-to? (Save them when you take the old drapes down at home! I KNOW they aren't available in the forest!!).

OK. You are now thinking about upgrading to a better shelter which offers much better protection from all sides and holds warmth far better than a lean-to. So just add another upright wall on the opposite side of the lean-to and create an A-Frame. The construction techniques are the same. Use the same materials for building and insulating.

SPACE is a huge consideration. Remember: you need space to at least sit up comfortably, store your gear, sleep in a bed long and wide enough so you can stretch out comfortably, and move around a bit without stooping over and banging your head all the time. The larger the space, the more heat required to warm it up in the cold. The optimum is to build a shelter which can retain heat AND provide adequate room. The more you can utilize a fire at a safe distance to provide some warmth, the more allowance you may have for that little bit of extra space.

Considering the fact that you'll likely have a much smaller door space to cover than in a lean-to, you won't require as much material to enclose the door. You WILL need adequate ventilation. I don't favour bring fire inside a shelter unless it has LARGE dimensions, like a well-constructed tipi which has a smoke hole in the top. This is a tricky tightrope walk. On the one hand, you want to ensure a flow of fresh air. On the other hand, you want protection from bugs and rain. That is why the use of mosquito netting may help if you leave enough space for ventilation and perhaps even fashion an "awning" (remember those, anyone??). If the sky is clear and red at night, you've listened to forecast and are ready just in case with more tarp material, concentrate on sealing the shelter against bugs. Your fire and insect repellent are your best friends here.

Wood has the advantage of being strong. It's worth your while finding branches that are strong, not brittle, especially for your ridgepole and for your bed. Use weaker branches, if you have to, on the walls, which bear less weight. Test your bed out before you lie down permanently for the night. It should EASILY hold your full weight PLUS. The cross pieces on your bed have to be strong.

Check for bugs, branches, and knots sticking out of the slats in your bed. Make sure the fire is dampened and not likely to "rise again in wrath", apply repellent, wind up the cat, put the clock out, and sleep. You need it if you're going to be busy with more tasks tomorrow. Wood shelters are fun to create as projects and dependable if properly constructed. Ideally, there'll be a mixture of hard wood and evergreen branches around. If you can, start building a wood shelter EARLY. You may have to expend more time than you had counted on surveying for materials. But you'll be really proud to have done a quality job!! Be confident. You CAN do this! Really, really well!

Your Pal,

Outdoors Guy

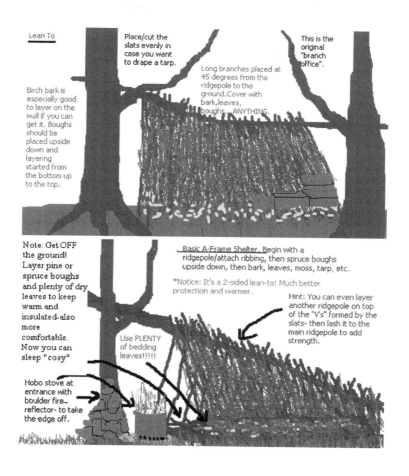

Lean To

Place/cut the slats evenly in case you want to drape a tarp.

This is the original "branch office".

Long branches placed at 45 degrees from the ridgepole to the ground. Cover with bark, leaves, boughs. ANYTHING.

Birch bark is especially good to layer on the wall if you can get it. Boughs should be placed upside down and layering started from the bottom up to the top.

Note: Get OFF the ground! Layer pine or spruce boughs and plenty of dry leaves to keep warm and insulated-also more comfortable. Now you can sleep "cosy"

Basic A-Frame Shelter. Begin with a ridgepole/attach ribbing, then spruce boughs upside down, then bark, leaves, moss, tarp, etc.

*Notice: It's a 2-sided lean-to! Much better protection and warmer.

Hint: You can even layer another ridgepole on top of the "V's" formed by the slats- then lash it to the main ridgepole to add strength.

Use PLENTY of bedding leaves!!!!!

Hobo stove at entrance with boulder fire- reflector- to take the edge off.

Snow, Snow, Beautiful Snow??

Before I begin this column, I'd like to say straight up that what follows here are some suggestions and strategies for building shelters. I haven't had as much practice with Winter shelters as I have shelters used in the other 3 seasons, so I want to start with a very basic idea. This idea is to either look for a space that affords natural shelter from cold, snow, and wind, or create that space in the snow. I offer 2 suggestions in this article- looking for an ever-green tree that has long branches for cover and then using it to create a shelter with a bed and additional wind protection, OR to dig a trench or pile up snow balls and then use cover for a roof, evergreen boughs as bedding, and improvise a weaved door to help keep out wind. (*I acknowledge that there are experts who have far more extensive knowledge and skills in Winter survival and certainly encourage anyone who wants to learn more to con-tinue reading and extending their knowledge.)

So it's snowed. Or let's say it's SNOWED. You need to get out of the elements as much as possible. You have to get out of the wind, stay dry, keep as warm as possible and find a way to get some rest and protection. I'm assuming a few things- you're properly dressed- lined boots, thermal socks, underwear, pants, mittens/gloves, hat/parka/balaclava, etc. This is first order stuff. It's what you have ON you to keep out cold.

There are so many decisions to make that. First, is there im-mediate danger or are you relatively safe and close to a road where you'll eventually get noticed? What do you have with you in your vehicle? What can you take from your surroundings? Certain principles are basic: warmth, water, whereabouts, weath-er (wind), wet/dry and "what's for dinner"? Think of them as the "W-6" considerations.

This article focuses on giving you a few more options besides staying with your vehicle (usually best option). After all, you may be hiking, in which case you may not be able to reach your vehicle in time before dark. Hope fully, you told people where you were going and what your expected time line was. Hopefully you've got your cell phone and it's CHARGED. Did you bring a space blanket, compass, water, nutrition bars, flashlight, whistle, belt knife, hatchet or folding saw... You'll at least have tools to work with.

Next: Shelter. The wind chill and the ground are 2 deadly enemies. You need to preserve as much body heat as you can, especially if conditions dictate you may have to wait out some bad weather. Here are 2 options.

1. The tree shelter. This can be tricky to find-just the "right" tree (not for Christmas either- this isn't a luxury). The evergreen tree with space underneath it's boughs for you and your gear. No branches sticking out with sharp edges. Branches must have thick enough cover to keep off most of the snow and block the wind. You're better starting off EARLY before light fails and you can't see to work. Clear snow from the area under the tree and pile it along the "walls"- under the outside perimeter of the lower boughs. You can add more snow for more protection and insulation from the wind. Layer the "floor" under the branches with as many dry leaves and pine/spruce boughs as you can. This is your bedding. Don't underestimate the amount of bedding you'll need. Layer it thickly to insulate you from the ground. Next, layer the walls with additional spruce boughs and pile up the snow. The door can also be improvised with a larger snowball and some spruce branches. At LEAST you're out of the direct wind and off the ground.

2. If the right tree has been sold, try this. Pile snow up (snowballs on top of each other) or dig a miniature bowling alley

into a large snow bank. Next step is the same as for the tree shelter-layer the floor. You'll need to collect some sturdy branches as slats to form a makeshift roof. If you can, slope it by running a larger branch down the center (perpendicular to) your wooden roof beams and layer spruce/pine boughs over it in a "v" shape. The steeper the "v", the more snow will slide off it instead of piling up ON it. A tarp or space blanket from your emergency kit would be awfully handy here as a roof/door. Finally: The doorway. You'll likely need that space blanket to roll up in. A tarp will do but has to be anchored. Here's a good idea. Get a hold of several limber branches and "weave" them into a portcullis type of design. If you can then get a few bundles of long grasses, weave them through the openings of the portcullis. You now have a makeshift door. Not as effective as the real medieval thing in keeping out the enemy, but you CAN wedge it into the snow and get some additional protection. If you need to, think IMPROVISE!! You can use your snowshoes or boughs as shovels or rakes (beats using your hands). Stomp a "V" or "SOS" in the snow. Lay down 2 logs in the shape of a "V" in a clearing. Build a fire for warmth and signalling. Use an ORANGE garbage bag as a makeshift flag or to cover your roof as a rescue signal. Hopefully, you'll have left some trail markings (surveyor's tape, broken branches) so people can track you. Text/call anyone you can and give them the best idea of your location using landmarks or bearings taken with your compass. A tip for water: you're better off carrying a water skin inside one of your layers rather than eating snow-which will burn valuable calories as your body warms it. With a water skin- the water is clean and warmer.

A FINAL NOTE: I acknowledge Les Stroud ("Survivorman") for this advice on the back cover of his book: *Survive:* "You sweat, you die." [1] You'll be working hard to build a shelter. Ok, it's cold, but if you've got layers on your body heat will build up. If your inner layers of clothing get wet, you are in serious trouble. There is no place to dry clothes. I must acknowledge the advice given by the experts. Layer down as you work. Stay DRY!! When you crawl into your shelter, you'll be far better off when you put the outer layers back on again.

[1]Stroud, Les, *Survive!* (Toronto: HarperCollins, 2008). Back Cover. *Quoted with permission.

Outdoors Guy

Snow "Hut" Dig a "bowling alley" in the snow bank. Use pine/spruce boughs for bedding. (You can even make a platform under your bed and insulate under and above it.) Lay slats over the "ceiling" and make the roof slanted to run off snow. A tarp or orange garbage bag (or space blanket) will keep out snow and serve to signal rescuers.

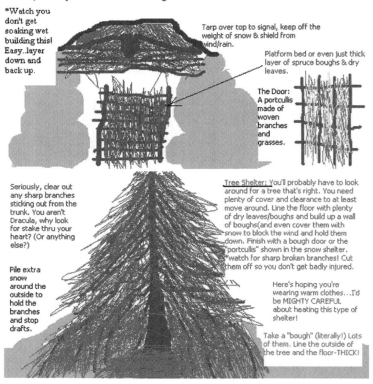

*Watch you don't get soaking wet building this! Easy..layer down and back up.

Tarp over top to signal, keep off the weight of snow & shield from wind/rain.

Platform bed or even just thick layer of spruce boughs & dry leaves.

The Door: A portcullis made of woven branches and grasses.

Seriously, clear out any sharp branches sticking out from the trunk. You aren't Dracula, why look for stake thru your heart? (Or anything else?)

Pile extra snow around the outside to hold the branches and stop drafts.

Tree Shelter: You'll probably have to look around for a tree that's right. You need plenty of cover and clearance to at least move around. Line the floor with plenty of dry leaves/boughs and build up a wall of boughs(and even cover them with snow to block the wind and hold them down. Finish with a bough door or the "portcullis" shown in the snow shelter. watch for sharp broken branches! Cut them off so you don't get badly injured.

Here's hoping you're wearing warm clothes...I'd be MIGHTY CAREFUL about heating this type of shelter!

Take a "bough" (literally!) Lots of them. Line the outside of the tree and the floor-THICK!

Vital Heat Retention

Survival is about the most very basic needs-at least to begin with. What does a human need to stay alive? Water, Air, Food, Protection, and Warmth. This doesn't say be comfortable. Just survive.

This also doesn't say that survival means limiting yourself to the basic elements either. You certainly can be comfortable or at least more comfortable. Limiting oneself in any way eliminates hope and purposeful activity. You want the BEST situation you can possibly achieve. Comfort, control over your immediate environment, a game plan, constant re-assessment and then goal-setting followed by ACTION. I'll cut this introduction short. Just imagine beginning a survival experience with nothing accomplished toward meeting your most basic needs. NOW imagine a well-constructed camp with bedding, a fire, a sturdy shelter which is secure from rain, wind, cold, strong sunlight, insects. Plentiful water you can purify and use, facilities to clean and cook, storage space, means of signaling, and some sources of food nearby.

You'd feel WAY cheered up! Situation two is WAY better than Situation One! This all takes time and effort...and that's a GREAT thing! You're busy without time to dwell on things. You have a clear purpose in mind, the knowledge and strategies and tools to keep moving in a positive direction.

The focus of this article is on one critical element of survival in cool/colder weather- warmth. There are 2 ways you can approach warmth. 1. The warmth you can CREATE. 2. The warmth you can RETAIN. Fire is absolutely CRITICAL in the wilderness. Perhaps nothing else will do as many things for you practically and psychologically as fire. But think about it. Heat is also a useless form of energy since a lot of heat ends up going off into the atmosphere. It isn't like chemical energy which can be converted into electrical energy or electrical energy which can be converted into light energy. Heat (unless you can harness enough of it to turn a turbine and generate electricity), warms us and then disappears. So the fundamental question is how to not only create it but to preserve it as efficiently and for as long as we can. The entire focus of this article, given the above background, is to discuss ways to conserve heat.

For the sake of space, please refer to suggestions made in previous articles involving the Hobo Heater, Biscuit Tin Stove, and Fire Can. These are designed, if you will, to produce sustained heat in a contained space. If a glowing coal or ember can be created, it is safer to use inside (or just outside) an A-Frame Shelter than an open fire. You can add just a few coals at a time to keep the heat radiating. To complement the radiating heat, insulation over the shelter in the form of pine/spruce branches is essential. Here the balance has to carefully maintained- you need enough warmth to take the chill away, but not enough to burn the house down.

Fire can be made more efficient with the construction of a fire reflector. I might even go so far as to suggest that you consider the following plan. If you have a lean-to constructed, enclose it on THREE sides. The front is exposed but we can improve the design here. Build a fire reflector with three walls to enclose the fire around the front of the lean-to. This has advantages. 1. It retains heat by radiation. The heat is reflected back towards you. 2. The wind is partially blocked which means some protection from smoke being blown at you and into your face. 3. You also have a wind-break to keep out colder winds. This design may also work facing the front of an A-Frame Shelter.

As mentioned in my Fire Article, feed your fire continuously. Don't pile the wood on all at once unless you've got a truck load. Firewood always burns faster than we think it will. Collect 6 times the fuel that you anticipate you'll need and use it steadily, bit by bit.

Burn it all at once and you can go sit in the cold. Watch for sparks. Hardwood burns longer and produces less sparks but takes longer to ignite- progress from dry softwood fuel to dry hardwood fuel.

Now to consider what you have that you must try to conserve as long as possible- body heat. The weather forecasters in my area always remind people to dress in layers in cold temperatures. Like so much else this discussion is based on simple physical principles. Heat travels in one of three ways- convection (moving air/water), conduction (so in this case we're talking about heat being sucked out of your body into the cold ground), and radiation. We've talked about re-radiating heat back towards you with a fire reflector.

To avoid losing heat by conduction, insulating you from the ground is important. Using leaves and boughs from evergreen trees provides insulation. This brings to light discussion about air. Air is a poor conductor, but a good INSULATOR- hence the idea of trapping dead air in-between layers of clothing. This same idea applies to insulation from the cold ground and rolling in a pile of dry leaves. Trap air in dead pockets and it will insulate you. The more insulation you can place down between yourself and the ground, the better. (Also, you are more comfortable!)

A few final thoughts and tips:

Take your clothes with you inside your sleeping bag and change inside the sleeping bag rather than crawling out into the cold and losing all the heat you've accumulated.

Look for quality fill for a sleeping bag. Down, Gore Tex™, and Dacron Hollofill™ have earned their reputation as quality insulators. **Important**! Keep the insulating material in your sleeping bag **DRY**! Down won't insulate when it becomes wet. You have to dry it out and re-fluff it so that it traps dead air again- and this is difficult in the cold weather!

A space blanket is made of shiny mylar and is used specifically to trap and re-radiate heat back towards your body. Carry 2 of them. DO NOT use them as fire reflectors. They aren't aluminum!

A "mummy bag" traps air into a more confined space than a rectangular sleeping bag. There is less space for your body to heat. However, you have less room to move around. You may wish to consider a mummy bag just a size bigger than your bodily dimensions.

Check the temperature rating for your sleeping bag and for your coat and boots! Then pack extra thermal shirts, socks, and even underwear. You can then add or subtract layers as needed and at the very least have one dry set of clothing to change into if you get wet by perspiring or, heaven forbid, getting dunked.

Foot and hand warmers, hexamine stoves and emergency candles can be life savers. Pack them.

Make sure to urinate before bed. Your body doesn't have to use keep to extra fluid warm.

Have a power snack before bed to generate some food energy/body warmth.

Mitts are warmer than gloves, all other things being equal.

Buy the best quality gear you can afford. Cheap, thin gear just isn't up to the job.

Remember to guard your HANDS, FEET, and HEAD, as so much body heat is lost thru these three areas due to the amount of blood flow to the surface of the skin.

Remember that your clothing, especially clothing next to your skin has to be kept dry. Pace yourself and adjust layers while working.

Don't bring clothing inside covered in snow. It melts you know.

Consider enclosing the front your A-Frame- even with a blanket. A woven portcullis door made from a branch frame and woven grasses and/or boughs can serve as a door to help keep out a draft.

Watch eating snow or drinking cold water. Your body expends calories to heat them up inside to body temperature.

Basic Idea Review:

Insulation- trap dead air with layers.

Use Radiation to reflect heat back towards you.

Reduce heat loss by conduction thru the ground by insulating yourself with bedding.

Stay DRY!

Make sound decisions about use of fuel with respect to availability of more fuel.

This all sounds exactly like what you'd do at home- home improvement- except that in THIS situation you're working by absolute necessity towards some relative measure of comfort. Make your home more heat efficient. Insulate. Play as many cards as you can to make your experience as warm and comfortable as possible. Have some materials with you like coals, a space blanket, lots of lighters and matches, a spare blanket, and emergency fire starters. Bring at least one complete change of dry clothes.

Hope You'll ALWAYS Be Safe!

Fire Reflector: The 2 uprights ("Y" Sticks) are drawn in black. Set them up by pushing them into the ground. Now use 2 uprights placed in the Y's and pushed into the ground. Simply stack branches as closely together as possible to form a wall. This helps reflect heat back towards you! The wider the better. I also used aluminum foil last year in place of the branches. Not bad, but flimsier. Building 2 walls together at angles helps retain more heat.

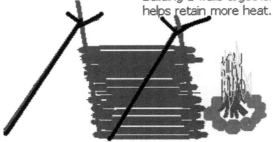

Note: The open part of your shelter faces the fire.

*Addendum- "Knotty, Knotty"

*Following is a list of knots for Camping, Fishing and Survival.

I've listed these knots as basic and trustworthy. Diagrams of these knots are easy to locate on line.

Bowline Knot- This is the one knot for outdoors and rescue that anyone should learn if they learn nothing else. Properly tied it will not slip or jam. This knot has multiple uses including hitching practically anything onto anything else or for dropping a rope down to someone who may be injured and stuck. *Make a single loop. The live end does this: "The rabbit runs out of its hole, runs behind the tree, and then runs back into the hole."

Taught Line Hitch- very secure and effective knot to attaching guy ropes for tent lines, hammocks, etc. It looks like a Double Overhand knot followed by a Single Overhand Knot- but not quite. It's WAY BETTER!

Clove Hitch- I can't describe this verbally. It is THE foundational knot for joining sections of braches together.

Loop Knot: Very secure for hitching your horse to the rails (just kidding). Make a loop and wind it twice around the rope. Pull tight. Good for mooring your canoe to a dock with a mooring fixture.

Blood Knot- Excellent for joining sections of rope or line.

Trilene Knot™- You've heard me mention this quite a few times. Why learn a whole pile of knots when one knot is so effective. It is, in my opinion, THE knot for tying line to a hook or to a swivel/snap-swivel. Check your line for nicks and frays, and re-tie occasionally. I do mention a few more knots for fishing, but this is where I usually go to do business.

Uni-Knot- Simply make a "U" when you pull your line thru the eye of a hook or swivel. Hold your hand at the top of the "U" and bring the live end up to it. Wind the line 6 times around your line, back up thru the loop, and pull tight. This looks (pardon me) like a noose at first. As you pull on the main line the knot travels down until it "locks". It'll "click". This knot, I've found, is better suited to 10 lb. plus line.

Uni-Snell- for typing trout and salmon hooks.

Albright Knot- Joins your fly backing line to the fly line very smoothly.

Improved Clinch Knot and San Diego Jam Knot- tested and effective fishing knots.

Connections, Reflections, and Recollections

I started out this book by saying that fishing hooked me when I was still very young. The outdoors got into my system when I was young. I had visions of long ago of me running thru the woods dressed in buckskins and wearing a coon skin cap. Imagined adventures flashed thru my mind. Some things never change. On a still morning out on the lake I still think those very same thoughts. Thankfully so much of nature still remains in Ontario.

This book has presented my connections to the outdoors. I've met some of the most amazing people- so many camp fires and so much laughter. We keep in touch during the winter e-mailing and Facebooking, counting down the days until we can return to camp. I've learned that each trip is a gift, and that each person you meet is a gift. We are a little community. Camping has taught me that we're all in this together. You learn to ask "if anybody needs anything in town." You learn that other people have their own stories. You also collect funny stories to look back and laugh about. Raccoons can really trash trailers and help themselves to the chips and cookies. I have nothing personally against them- they're just trying to survive like we are. Having said that... I've been inadvertently called out on raccoon duty in the middle of the night to try and chase them away and then cleaned up after these, "Weapons of Mess Destruction" swept thru a hapless trailer or entered (uninvited) into a dining tent. The important thing is that my friends would help me out too- in a heartbeat. The groundskeeper at camp went to the trouble of opening the camp for me when I had to travel north on short notice to attend to a sick family member.

I'm often called upon to fix things while camping. I bring so much "stuff" with me- yet it all packs down neatly into my SUV. I've learned how to improvise- the subject of 5 of my articles.

There is always the lure of another fish. This just never goes away. If I were a computer this would be on the hard drive. Add to that the challenge of new outdoors projects. There is ALWAYS a new skill and/or idea to try. My bemused friends have watched me build shelters and my "Totally Improv Camp". Yet they passed on positive words. I am known as "Basic Bob". I like the title.

The more trips you make "up North", the more memories you accumulate. I had a fish jump out of the water from the left side of the canoe, swipe my face, and land with a splash in the water on the right side of the canoe. Strange…but it really DID happen. I went up camping in May thinking, "It's May- no need for winter boots." 2 days later it SNOWED- 3 inches of WET slush- and me in a tent. It got COLD and I was in the driver's seat of my SUV, bundled up in every layer you can imagine. The next day it was off to the outdoor store to buy winter boots.

Then there was the infamous shower. The water had just been hooked up but for some strange reason it was running the wrong way thru the filters. There was a chemical of some kind in the shower water. Combined with soap, it formed some kind of glue. No, I'm not kidding. I thought it was some joke shop kind of soap so I showered again and added another layer of goo to my skin and hair. Then, there being nothing else for it, I went into the newly iced out lake to wash again (twice) to get the goo off.

A thieving rogue (raccoon) had the nerve to steal a freshly caught walleye from my picnic table. I ran after the scoundrel but it was faster. The next day I found my fish chain-minus 1 walleye. The neighbours really got a kick out of the chase. I also found out that raccoons are aficionados of margarine. Again, you learn by being careless. A whole POUND of margarine disappeared into the belly of but ONE raccoon. I was hoping that indigestion would avenge me.

Turtles have helped themselves to a couple of my fish. Moral of the story- don't leave fish chained to dock. I've fallen out of the canoe (once) in full view of the kids. My tent was stored in the back shed only to be opened up at the campsite with a huge hole rotted thru the back wall- a perfect invitation for mosquitoes (and, yes, they did show up).

One memorable event took place at the local community church. I was at the Sunday Service and they just HAPPENED to announce that they were giving away margarine to anyone that might want it. (Maybe there was a surplus from a church luncheon?) I just HAPPENED to have forgotten to pack margarine.

These are all, "You'll look back and laugh at this someday" happenings. I do look back and laugh. Hopefully, you'll have your own set of stories to tell.

The lure of fresh coffee, bacon frying, the sun rising and setting, beautiful scenery, the absolute quiet and also the songs from birds, not to mention the sites of natural landmarks, just have a way of beckoning us to return.

This book was written to provide knowledge and skills to just, hopefully, make your experiences a bit richer and to extend your knowledge. It was written to give ideas you can try. Trying a new shelter or Improv idea has a way of making me feel creative and alive. My brain gets going and I get enthused. What a terrific feeling! Then- spoiled brat- I get to look at my "creation", feel proud of it, and take a photo. Knowledge is a great thing because we have more we can use at our disposal. Then there are the situations where you may need that knowledge- and where you'll be glad you prepared ahead of time and brought the right equipment to handle the situation and stay "on top".

If I may end somewhere close to where I began- preparation is essential. Then embellish preparation with some skill at improvising. There are so many things you can use certain items for. You are a capable person. You can look at an "ordinary" item like a tarp, a coat hanger, a coffee can, or a garbage bag (orange) and see what can be.

My love for the outdoors has brought me so many non-monetary benefits. My family and students I've taught have bought me so many wonderful gifts knowing my love for the outdoors. My family have also been encouraging and supportive of this project. They wish me a safe trip every time I go camping and we text each other. My diet remains a friendly, "we agree to disagree" situation. Eating dandelion and plantain salad, clams, arrowheads and cattails, and the occasional berries, along with canned macaroni, beans and stew may not suit people's every-day diet. To my credit, I DO pack potatoes and onions for grilling fish.

I hope you've enjoyed the book and picked up a few ideas along the way. If you experience some increase in your success rate fishing, great. If you've learned how to improvise for what you may have forgotten to pack, great. If you are reminded to pack carefully and plan ahead for that hike, great. If you are stuck and have the resources- both material and mental, great. If you just plain enjoy the outdoors a bit more, GREAT!!

It has been a PLEASURE sharing what I've learned with you.

God Bless You. Have fun. Be safe. I'd like to wish everyone warm, sunny weather, memorable moments, fun and friends, photos, projects, outdoor meals, and campfires.

Happy Trails.

Outdoors Guy

Photos

Cookin' a la Improv-
Fire Can & Fry Pan

Tripod Bed With A-Frame Tarp Roof-Comfort and Shade

Comforts of Home (Leaves piled high...) Note the tripod, candles, "tent", bench, & fire pit.

A Lean-To

An A-Frame- Ready for Layering with Bark, Leaves, and Boughs

Basic Tarp Tent- DON'T set one up in the Direction of the Wind!!

Using a makeshift rake/broom- easier this way... Stoves are on the Table

Totally Improv Camp By Night

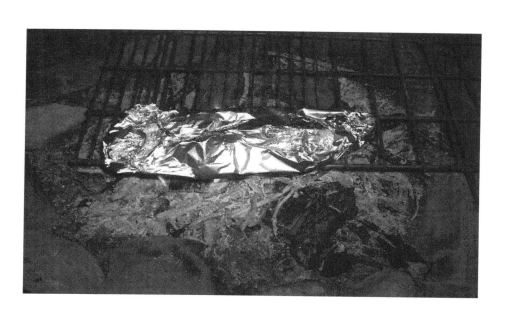

Fish a la Grille- So Good!!

Firing Up The Hobo Heater

Aluminum Foil Fire Reflector

The Noble Art of
Baitcasting- Results!! = ☺

Teepee Fire- Simple and Effective Heat Source

Fire Tinder- Tinder Fungus (Black), Dead Birch Bark, Dried Pine Needles, Dryer Lint

Improv Bench-Tripods, 2 Long Poles, Grill Racks and Pine Boughs

Cross Hatch Fire- Constructed During the Daytime- Ready For Night's Festivities

The Noble Art of Baitcasting- Strikes Again!! = ☺

Made in the USA
Charleston, SC
01 June 2014